VENCHI

CHOCOLATE SOMMELIER

A JOURNEY THROUGH THE CULTURE OF CHOCOLATE

WHITE STAR PUBLISHERS

NINE OUT OF TEN PEOPLE LOVE CHOCOLATE,
THE TENTH LIES.

- *John Tullius* -

An advertisement from the beginning
of the 20th century of French
company Delespaul-Havez
(1848-1976).

TEXTS BY CLARA AND GIGI PADOVANI

PHOTOGRAPHS BY FABIO PETRONI

RECIPES BY RELAIS CUBA CHOCOLAT

Project Editor VALERIA MANFERTO DE FABIANIS

Editorial Assistant GIORGIO FERRERO

Graphic Design MARIA CUCCHI

CONTENTS

RECOGNIZED BENEFICIAL EFFECTS

FIVE SENSES FOR TASTING

PERFECT HARMONY

HAPPY IN CHOCOLATE

They have called us the "chocolate couple" of food writing. And indeed, for many years our passion for chocolate has taken us to various parts of the world, to learn about the different processes, to discover its secrets and to learn how to taste it, identifying its organoleptic peculiarities. We have visited traditional artisan's workshops, factories equipped with modern machinery, museums dedicated to the Food of the Gods and cocoa plantations. Yet, whenever we unwrap a chocolate bar, choose a praline, sip a cup of hot chocolate, sink a teaspoon into a cream spread, taste a slice of chocolate cake, we always immerse ourselves into the magical world linked to this food, which is so different from any other. It is seductive, voluptuous, sensual, and fulfilling.

It's true, the similarities with the world of wine are strong, but the smile that spontaneously lights up the faces of those who are tasting *Theobroma cacao* is unparalleled. The history of chocolate is very ancient, but for the developed world it is quite recent. Yet the influence it has had on social life, literature and art make us understand how chocolate has a "differential" of pleasure and joy that perhaps no other food can offer.

As we bite into a chocolate bar and it slowly melts in our mouths, our taste buds receive complex notes, different for each cocoa *cru*. The scent is wild, aromatic, evocative. You can sense an ancestral call to the Amazon rainforest where the first pod was born, to exotic flowers, to hints of wood and coffee. The taste of vanilla or sugar should not prevail, as they are an indication of a low-percentage cocoa mass. The taste is addictive, with some references of bitterness and acidity that accentuates its complexity.

A good quality chocolate should not be eaten but tasted. The surprise arrives a few minutes after tasting: more than five hundred aromatic notes spread like a harmonious symphony across our palate, to be followed by a long pleasure activated by salivation on the sides of the tongue.

Oscar Wilde wrote that "anything in life that's any fun is either immoral, illegal or fattening." However, the Food of the Gods has been an exception for centuries. *Chocolat et santé* are two inseparable factors and many French doctors of the 19th century were already convinced of this. Today, the most recent scientific researches have shown that the moderate but continuous consumption of dark chocolate gives health benefits to the brain, heart, and to the arteries. Instead, the positive influences concerning mood... well, you've probably already found them out for yourself.

Marcel Proust praised the "chocolate creams light and fleeting": it isn't necessary to reread his pages of *Recherche* dedicated to the "madeleines" to highlight how indelible our childhood memory is in imprinting the taste of chocolate. To be honest, the two of us belong to the generation who had a rather tormented relationship with this food: the object of desire, as children, was often bestowed sparingly by mothers, convinced that it was a food able to satisfy only gluttony, which brought out pimples – a false accusation – or that made you fat – depends, but it is not true. Therefore, the concession of the chocolate bar to bite, modeled like a tank, accompanied always by bread, was an exception of the snacks of the early Sixties.

Then, it arrived, the mythical cream spread born in Alba (the city where we grew up immersed in the scent of toasted hazelnuts and cocoa), which cleared chocolate's name, conquering Italian and European moms. For the years of our adolescence, just the presence of the jar on the top shelf of the pantry was enough to reassure us and make us "happy." But then, growing up and discovering the seductive world of the Food of the Gods, we finally became "happy in chocolate."

You can be happy in chocolate without spending too much. Carole Matthew, author of English romance novels, wrote: "whoever said money couldn't buy you happiness clearly didn't spend their cash on chocolate."

But just loving chocolate isn't enough, you also have to know it. Indeed, we believe that a true chocolate "sommelier," that is a connoisseur, must retrace the wonderful history of this food, which is five thousand years old, but also discover the mysterious raw material with which it is made: cocoa. Do you have any idea how a bar is produced? It is a long and complex workmanship, in some ways magical, that can allow us to understand how much passion man gives to the alchemical transformation of those brown seeds from distant lands. Moreover, how many types of chocolate are there? Just three, or is the range broader?

What are the most famous chocolates and cakes that have conquered the most enthusiastic palates? Perhaps you will be amazed to learn about *Theobroma cacao*'s healthy properties, which have been recognized by indisputable scientific sources, or to read about the phases of a perfect tasting involving the five senses, which resemble that of wine. And also, what do you drink with gianduia or with a dark chocolate? Which are the best spice combinations?

Fabio Petroni's extraordinary photographs that illustrate this book will certainly light up the passion of all you *chocoholics* out there, just like the recipes by Relais Cuba Chocolat will make you want to try out some of the dishes and cocktails for yourself. On our part, we have tried to satisfy every curiosity about the Food of the Gods, hoping that our narrative will lead you in this wonderful universe, to remain always, like us, happy in chocolate. This expression can give you an idea of the joy of slowly dissolving a chocolate in your mouth, remembering the scents of a patisserie, or the first hot chocolate tasted on a cold winter evening, or to the emotion, for those who have had the chance to experience it, of walking through a plantation with the yellow or red pods popping up from the trunks. So, abandon your guilt and let yourself be happily conquered by *Theobroma cacao*, the greediest gift of the Gods to men.

FIVE THOUSAND
YEARS OF HISTORY

When we bite into a chocolate bar or we let a praline melt in our mouths our brains immediately receive a sense of pleasure, which is altogether relaxing and stimulating and which is called *indulgence*: the satisfaction of the senses. Nowadays chocolate is an everyday pleasure, it's an easily accessible food that everybody can afford. But it hasn't always been so. For centuries, only the world's élite could enjoy this delight that comes from cocoa: it was the sublime "companionship" drink sipped by the aristocrats of the European Courts and, even before then, it was an energetic potion drunk by the leaders of pre-Columbian civilizations. It was originally consumed in its liquid state. Chocolate became solid, democratic and cheap only after 1849, in the United Kingdom, when J.S. Fry & Sons company – founded in Bristol in 1761 by Quaker capitalists – created the first bar of a *Chocolat Délicieux à Manger*. The long history of the Food of the Gods is full of "conventional fairy tales," but there is one indisputable truth: the first drink made by men from toasting and beating up seeds extracted from a strange colored fruit in the shape of a football was made in the American Continent. It happened many years before Christopher Columbus took the wrong route with his ships while searching for a new way to India. And it is proven that it arrived in Europe from the lands of New Spain along with the treasures that had been raided from the *conquistadores*, in the 16th century. Initially the Europeans refused this beverage, since it was cold, sour and spicy, so much that in 1565 the Tuscan traveler Girolamo Benzoni defined it as a "pig's beverage" in his *Historia del Mondo Nuovo*. So, it became a medicine. Later it was served hot and sugared and it was enhanced by the followers of exoticism during the *Ancien Régime*, along with tea and coffee. Finally, from the mid-1800s, resourceful craftsmen and industrial chocolate makers from the UK, Turin and Switzerland were able to create brilliant products to satisfy the sweet tooth of the Middle-classes.

18 - One of the first illustrations of a cocoa tree, taken from Historia del Mondo Nuovo *by Girolamo Benzoni.*

19 - Cocoa harvesting painted on a Sèvres porcelain vase (1827): it depicts the cutting of the pods with a machete.

A GIFT FROM THE GODS

There is a myth dating back to the Aztecs about the origins of chocolate. The pre-Colombian civilization, which emerged in the 14th century in Mexico, had complex cosmology theories. Their books tell of how this very precious plant was given to men by a god: the "Star of the morning, the Breath of life, the Precious Twin, the Quetzal-feathered Serpent," already king and leader of the Toltecs. Everything about that city state – developed from the 14th to the 16th century – was regulated according to rituals of sacrifice and ceremonies in which cocoa had an essential role, besides being a store of value.

The Spanish wrote these things in their traveling journals about the New World, and so that magical aura given to chocolate by the Mesoamerican populations was received with restraint and suspicion by the Europeans. It was only in the mid-1700s, two centuries later, that a Swedish scientist gave the "chocolate plant" a scientific name. It was the famous botanist Linnaeus (Carl Nilsson Linnaeus, 1707-1778) who introduced the two-term naming system in botany and in the 1758 edition of his *Systema Naturae* he described a strange American plant and he assigned this plant the *Theobroma* (Food of the Gods) genus and the *cacao* species. Since then, everyone called *Theobroma cacao* those exotic "almonds" that were able to develop celestial flavors.

The Quetzalcoatl cult is described to us by the Bernandino de Sahagun in his *Historia universal de las cosas de Nueva España*, written around 1576. It's a monumental work: the Franciscan wrote twelve volumes about the cult, in Spanish and in *nahualt*, which was the Aztec's language. It's a richly illustrated manuscript with about two thousand pictures made by indigenous people and it gives us a very vivid idea of religious rituals and of social life, captured by the eyes of native Mexican people.

It tells of how Quetzalcoatl, after realizing that his peoples' food was too poor, wanted to give the Aztecs a plant that was able to give precious fruits from which they could obtain a sour and spicy beverage, full of energetic and aphrodisiac properties, named *xo-coatl*. The story goes that a Mexican princess had been left to guard a treasure by her husband, while he was away fighting to defend the empire.

20 - Aztec statue of a man holding a cabosse in his hand.

21 - An Aztec calendar (Codex Fejervary-Mayer) *with the drawing of a cocoa plant in a cardinal point (on the right).*

In his absence, she was assaulted by enemies who tried to make her reveal the hiding place of the treasure. She wouldn't talk and so was killed in revenge. From the blood that spilled from her grew a little cocoa plant, and it was in its fruit that the real treasure was hidden: seeds – as sour as the pain of love; seeds – as strong as virtue; seeds – barely pink like the blood of that faithful woman. The God Quetzalcoatl then gave cocoa to men as a present and as a reminder of the loyalty of the princess.

According to the legend, the feathered god with the white beard then left his homeland and descended amongst the mortals. When Spanish explorer Hernàn Cortés arrived in Mexico, the Aztecs thought he was Quetzalcoatl's incarnation and they honored him with jewels and cocoa seeds. Besides mythology, from written documents, crafted artifacts and devotion objects found in archeological digs we know that cocoa was very important in specific moments, such as births, weddings and in the cult of the dead.

AN AMAZONIAN BEVERAGE

It's always been thought that the birth-place of cocoa was the Mesoamerican area between Southern Mexico (Yucatan Peninsula, the States of Chiapas, Tabasco, Oaxaca) Belize, Guatemala and Honduras. These statements were supported both from the reports of the *conquistadores* and from archeological findings, although they were in contrast with botanical studies which place the growth of the wild cocoa plant in the wet lands of the Amazonian forest, and so much farther south, between Ecuador, Peru and Brazil. A recent finding has confirmed what the naturalists stated: traces of the Food of the Gods have been found in digs that were carried out in Santa Ana-La Florida, in the south of Ecuador. Hence it was a Mayo-Chinchipe, a population that took their name from the local rivers, the first man to drink chocolate.

The news, reported in November 2018 by the American scientific magazine *Nature Ecology & Evolution*, caused a shock among the experts. Archeologist Michael Blake, from the British Colombia University in Vancouver, Canada, was surprised by some decorated vases found in the digs at 500 miles (800 km) south of Ecuador's capital Quito, in Podocarpus National Park, almost at the border with Peru. These vases had clear traces of a dark liquid: the tests done by archeologists from the Canadian expedition revealed that it was in fact cocoa, that could be dated back to a time period from 5300 to 2100 years ago. Thanks to this discovery it was possible to backdate the first human consumption of the cocoa plant to two thousand years before.

Other diggings in Honduras, conducted by American researchers led by American archeologist Rosemary Joyce, from Berkeley, have brought to light other vases with traces of cocoa dating back to three thousand years ago. Are they seeds coming from plantations or wild plants? In this regard Joyce prefers the first option, while she's convinced that Ecuadorian populations in Santa Ana, did not start to grow cocoa but just cooked the fava beans from the wild fruits of the rainforest. To support this theory there is proof that the genetic fingerprinting of cocoa's "domestication" has been found in Central America.

22 - Lid of a Mayan vase (600-900 A.D.) found in Guatemala, depicting the deity of cocoa.

So, there is still a great mystery: how did the cocoa beans make a journey of thousands of miles from the Amazon rainforest to the Mesoamerican highlands? *Theobroma* beans are not fertile any more after being harvested and stored.

This is shown by the fact that, when the Spanish and the Portuguese transferred the plantations from Mexico to Africa, they had to eradicate living plants from the soil, transporting them on ships and replanting them: of course, a very difficult practice to adopt a thousand years before Christ.

OLMECS, MAYANS, AZTECS: THE FIRST CONSUMERS

According to anthropological and historical studies, there are three main Meso-American populations for which there is testimony of the use of cocoa: Olmecs, Mayans and Aztecs.

The most ancient are the Olmecs, who were settled not very far from what is known today as Mexico City. Their culture blossomed around 1200 B.C. and lasted about five centuries. We know very little about this population, as there is only little written testimony, but the archeological findings show that their art expression was very refined. Their diet was made up essentially of corn *tortillas*, while the women, who after giving birth needed proteins and fats to breast-feed their children, finished their meals with an energetic infusion based on cocoa beans, that were dried and finely chopped.

Later, in Yucatan and Guatemala, the Mayan civilization developed and reached its pinnacle between 300 and 900 A.D. The Franciscan bishop Diego De Lauda – sadly known to have destroyed almost all their books – wrote in his diary, drawn up in Spain in 1566, that the local habit was to make a beverage with shredded corn and cocoa, which had foam and was "very salty." After all sugar didn't exist yet, in fact it arrived to the New Continent from Spain.

Despite the Spanish inquisition, some of the Mayan books were stored in the Dresden Codex: in these books there are depictions of Mayans holding plates full of cocoa beans and from the text it has been possible to decode the writing *u kakaw*, the first etymology for the cocoa plant.

In a Mayan tombstone discovered in 1984 in Rio Azul, Guatemala, fourteen ceramic dishes and six cylindrical finely decorated vases on a pedestal were brought to light. One of these vases, now stored at the Princeton Art Museum in New Jersey, depicts the complex beverage preparation ceremony: they poured the liquid from one vase, held at about 3 feet in height, to another one placed on the ground, so that the foam would form.

This same operation is still used in Latin America but it is made with a *molinillo*, a small wooden whisk, which is similar to the device to remove air bubbles from champagne, and was introduced by the *conquistadores*.

In the 13th century, the Aztecs put the Mayans under their rule and learned how to use cocoa from them.

25 left – A vase with traces of cocoa from five thousand years ago, found in Santa Ana–La Florida, Ecuador.

25 right – A ritual container for cocoa came to light in a Maya tomb during the excavations in Rio Azul, Guatemala.

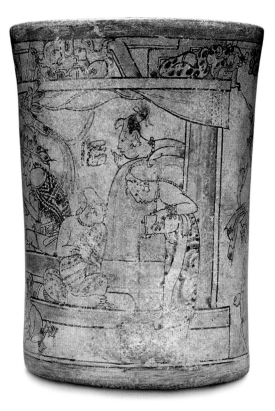

American husband and wife Sophie and Michael Coe have studied the pre-Colombian civilizations for years and in their book *The True Story of Chocolate* (1996) they claim the Mayans and Aztecs created a "varied and complicated beverage assortment, from floured ones, to *porridges*, powder and probably even solid ones, and to each of them they could add a wide variety of aromas."

The Aztecs also started to stock up on the beans: they were used as money in the city-state capital Tenochtitlan (where the present-day Mexico City is), where 960 million beans were stored. The dark seeds became a store of value and were even falsified, made out of earth and wax, which proves how precious they actually were.

The Spanish officer, Bernal Díaz del Castillo in his book, published after his death in 1632, *Historia verdadera de la conquista de la Nueva España*, reports about an Aztec feast attended by Emperor Montezuma: "From time to time they served him some cups with a beverage made of cocoa, which they said was useful for making a good impression on women." The book also describes the large quantity served to the king: "I saw them taking more than 50 big vases prepared with foam, of good cocoa, and he drank it; and the women served it with great respect…" Everyone at the royal palace made a great use of it, maybe not in such large quantities: everyday two thousand cups of that dark foamy liquid were made, destined to the royal guard soldiers.

The first encounter between Europeans and chocolate took place in 1502 off the coast of the island of Guanaja, when the natives brought some cups of a drink which Christopher Columbus did not even taste, turning up his nose at it. Eighty long years went by before a consistent load of dried seeds was shipped from Veracruz in Mexico to Seville, where it arrived only in 1585. And from that moment onwards the history of chocolate changed.

26 top - The Maya vase depicting the ritual of the cocoa drink poured from above, stored at Princeton.

26 bottom - A traditional molinillo, *wooden utensil to form foam in hot chocolate.*

27 - Stone table depicting a Maya priest paying homage to a cocoa plant.

Folio 305

Americain auec Sa Chocolatiere et Son Gobelet

Rameau de L'arbre du Cacao

Cacao

Gousses de vanille

TO THE CONQUEST OF EUROPEAN PARLORS

The "discovery" of America caused a real disruption to food habits on both continents of the Atlantic shores. Native Mexican cuisine almost completely lacked in fat, being made mainly of corn-based *tortillas* and *tamales*, because corn was the most common crop, while Europeans in the Iberian Peninsula, who ate a lot of meat and fish, didn't like the food of the *indios*, as they called them. Hence the Mexican started to breed cattle, milk cows, sheep, goats, pigs and chickens – imported from Europe – and learned to cook them. Then they discovered cane sugar: neither Mayans nor Aztecs loved sweet food, even though they knew about honey. It was still years before potatoes would reach, and feed the people of Northern Europe and the tomato those of Southern Europe.

After the Spanish conquest of South America, however, a slow "hybridization" came about between customs and traditions thanks to the women: many Mexican women married or went to serve Spanish men and learned to cook and to prepare what we now call "fusion" food. The missionary nuns of Gjajaca (Oaxaca) were probably the first to warm and stir up the crushed cocoa beans with sugar, making a chocolate much more similar to the one we eat nowadays. But at least until 1580 the Spanish continued to drink it sour, and strictly cold. Indeed, it seemed really undrinkable to the first travelers. And so, in his work, Benzoni wrote: "It [chocolate] looks like a beverage for pigs more than men [...] Its taste is quite bitter, it sates and refreshes the body, but it doesn't get it drunk, and this is the best, the most priceless good that the Indians honor and consume."

It was a doctor from Toledo, Francisco Hernández, who led the first scientific expedition to New Spain to study all the different botanic varieties that where unknown to Europe. He stayed in America for seven years, from 1570 onwards, and he described the flora and fauna in a monumental work entitled *Historia de las Plantas de Nueva España* made up of fifteen volumes. Hernández wrote about cocoa and chocolate, saying that the *cacahoatl* seeds were used to prepare a drink, because the local populations "had not yet discovered how to make wine;" these seeds were extracted from an oblong plant similar to a melon, but "striped and red colored." The doctor wrote: "The blackish seeds are made of a tender substance, very nourishing, slightly sour but at the same time a bit sweet, naturally warm or slightly cold and moist."

It seems the first cocoa seeds were brought to Spain by missionaries: it could have been the Franciscan father Olmedo, or more likely the Cistercian father Jeronimo Aguilera, who was in Cortès' expedition. When he got back to Europe, Aguilera delivered a little treasure of seeds to don Antonio de Alvaro, the prior of the Piedra monastery, in Aragon, near Zaragoza. According to tradition, this monastery was actually the first place in Europe in which hot chocolate was prepared, in 1524. The monks had suddenly become enthusiastic supporters of the beverage, spreading the recipe: in little "secret" rooms above the cloisters of the monasteries, the nourishing, warm delight was prepared.

So, the new nectar, dark and inviting, traveled from church to church, but also from noble house to noble house, from court to court: in the beginning it was considered as a kind of drug, but then it became a medicine which was appreciated for its flavor, for the stimulating properties it had and for its supposed therapeutic virtues.

Warm, scented, sweet: the "wild" roots of chocolate had already been forgotten and, thanks to the Spanish, chocolate started to conquer the Old Continent. First in Flanders, then in France thanks to dynastic weddings: it was women who especially fell in love with it. Tools were made to serve it: from the chocolate pot equipped with a hole for the wooden whisk to mix it before serving, to the various shaped cups, some which came with a metal handled little tray to prevent them from falling over: the tool was named "mancerina" in honor of its inventor, the first marquis of Mancera, don Pedro Alvarez de Toledo y Leiva (1585-1634), viceroy of Peru. From that kind of tool, which was useful also to avoid staining the precious dresses of the dames, later on, in the 1700s, they invented the *trembleuses*, long and narrow cups, slightly flared at the top, held by a ring to the plate.

30 - A silver chocolate pot in George II style (circa 1730).

31 - An illustration taken from the Codex Tudela *(1553) depicting an Aztec noblewoman preparing chocolate.*

CHOCOLATE SOMMELIER

*32 top left - A French chocolate pot in 18th century silver,
the work of Master Pierre Vallières.*

*32 bottom right - A German-produced chocolate pot in Meissen
ceramic (1735/1740).*

*33 top left - A ceramic chocolate pot from 1780 made by the Vinovo
factory (Piedmont, Italy).*

*33 bottom right - An American chocolate pot in silver with ivory
whisk (1860-1874), by Ball, Black & Co.*

34 top left - An Austrian trembleuse *cup by*
Du Paquier (Vienna, circa 1740).

34 bottom right - A French trembleuse *in Sévres*
porcelain (1776), by Étienne-Jean Chabry.

35 top - An elegant Viennese chocolate set,
with porcelain and glass cups, with gold handles
(circa 1735).

35 bottom - A trembleuse *with floral design without*
handles, made in Vienna.

For many years, preparing a good chocolate remained a "Spanish secret," but the monopoly was soon broken. The first one to succeed in Italy was traveler Francesco d'Antoni Carletti, at the Medici court: he visited San Salvador and Guatemala in 1600, where he saw cocoa plantations and, once he returned to Florence in 1606, he showed his scientific report in the form of a manuscript to Ferdinando I de' Medici, Grand Duke of Tuscany. The study was published only a hundred years later, but it had been consulted by scientist and doctor Francesco Redi who wrote about it in his *Bacco in Toscana*, capturing the interest of Grand Duke Cosimo III.

In baroque times especially, jasmine chocolate was very popular and it was only made in Florence. In those years *Theobroma cacao* made its appearance in

Turin too, probably in honor of the dynastic wedding celebrated in 1585 between the eighteen-year old Catherine Michelle of Spain, daughter of Philip II, and Savoy Duke Carlo Emanuele I: even though there are no written proofs, the "Spanish etiquette" imported from the bride probably included the "Indian broth," as hot chocolate was called back then.

In a few years time, from the mid-1600s to the beginning of the 1700s, the Food of the Gods contributed to the change of social costumes and traditions: while coffee, cheaper and easier to prepare, was conquering the new middle-classes, chocolate found its place in the parlors of gallant men and ladies in waiting for its sweet sensuality.

*36-37 - A Catalan mosaic in azulejos
ceramics dedicated to a noble
"La Xocolatada" feast (Barcelona, 1710).*

France was captured right away, thanks to the wedding between two very young royals: Anna of Austria, daughter of Philip III, king of Spain and the French king Louis XIII of Bourbon. Cardinal Richelieu first and then Maria Theresa, Louis XIV's wife since 1659, adapted it to Versailles. The first "licence" to dispense *une certeine composition qui si nomme chocolat* is reported in that year, and was accorded to the *maître chocolatier* David Chaillou. Maria Theresa herself said: "my only loves are chocolate and the king."

The Dutch, being good navigators, managed to take away cocoa's trading monopoly from the Spanish. From 1634 to 1728, Amsterdam became the main center of importation in North Europe, thanks to the Guipúzcoa Company, while Nice (which was a Savoy city back then) and Seville were the centers for the South. The Dutch were also responsible for spreading the habit of drinking hot chocolate outside the Spanish ecclesiastical areas.

Theobroma cacao reached Germany in 1641 thanks to a naturalist from Nuremberg, Johann Georg Volkammer, who returning from a trip to Italy suggested it as an aphrodisiac.

38 - The Christmas Day breakfast of 1762, in the apartment of Empress Maria Theresa of Austria, painted by Archduchess Maria Christina.

But it was the Dutch Cornelius Bontekoe, who lived in Berlin as a court doctor, to promote its use as a medicine by publishing his discussions on tea and chocolate (1678).

In those same years, chocolate arrived in England after coffee (from Africa) and tea (from Asia): the first coffee house to be known opened in 1650 in Oxford and it served all three of the exotic beverages, while in 1657 the first cocoa house opened in London, and it was managed by a French man. The British Dominican Thomas Cage, with his work called *New Survey of the West Indies* (1648) contributed to the etymological knowledge of the term *chocolate*: in the Aztec language *atl* means "liquid" but it also refers to the sound that water makes when it is mixed in a bowl with cocoa.

We can state that from the mid-1600s onwards the whole of Europe was conquered by the drink made with cocoa, even though it was still only limited to noble palaces and other few public halls attended by intellectuals and artists.

39 - The famous painting by Jean-Baptiste Charpentier le Vieux, entitled "The Cup of Chocolate" (1768).

MEDICAL AND THEOLOGICAL DISPUTES

Before they became commonplace, those piping hot cups of chocolate were welcomed skeptically by some and enthusiastically by others. Disputes began to take place between doctors, who were divided between those who believed chocolate was good to cure a lot of diseases and those who considered it to be an evil food. The first work to analyze the therapeutic virtues of cocoa was written in Mexico by a doctor at the court of Philip II, father Augustin Farfán, who, in 1592, wrote the *Tratado breve de medicina y de todas las enfermedades que a cada passo se ofrecen*. The augustinian father believed that cocoa was useful to cure breast chapping on postpartum women and suggested it as a laxative – if consumed in a cup in the morning – and to get rid of kidney stones.

Soon a heated debate begun, especially in Spain, with many treaties one against the other. The Andalusian Bartolomeo Marradón, in 1616, blamed chocolate to be the source of occlusions and dropsy (liquid accumulation). In 1631, Antonio Colmenero de Ledesma answered with his *Curioso tratado de la naturaleza y calidad del chocolate*, which soon became a best-seller, and he also attached a recipe to reveal the "Spanish secret": among all the confusion of those who believed that it made people fat and those who believed it made the stomach stronger, those who believed it could warm and inflame the body and those who drank it at every hour because they felt better, doctor Colmenero decided not to condemn a drink that was "so good and so healthy." From that moment, several books were published in favor of chocolate, such as that of Englishman Henry Stubbes, in 1662, with the significant title *The Indian Nectar*, and the text published in France on initiative of a merchant from Lyon, who in doing so also advertised his own activities: *De l'usage du caphé, du thé et du chocolat (1671)*.

But the health issue was not the only source of controversy surrounding the Food of the Gods. In the old continent, between the end of the 1500s and the mid-1600s, another dispute begun, a religious one: did that drink, which was so energetic, interrupt the ecclesiastical fasting or not? That is, was it to be considered a simple liquid, and so admitted in the church's doctrine, or was it an actual food?

The strongest supporters of the "Indian broth" were the Jesuits, the biggest monastic order of Christianity, founded in Spain on the initiative of Ignatius of Loyola. In the 1600s, the Jesuits had created a powerful army of believers, made of 16,000 monks and they were able to undertake permanent missions in Brazil, Paraguay and especially in Mexico, near the cocoa plantations.

41 - The Book of Spanish historian Antonio de León Pinelo (1636) dedicated to the "moral problem" of ecclesiastical fasting and chocolate.

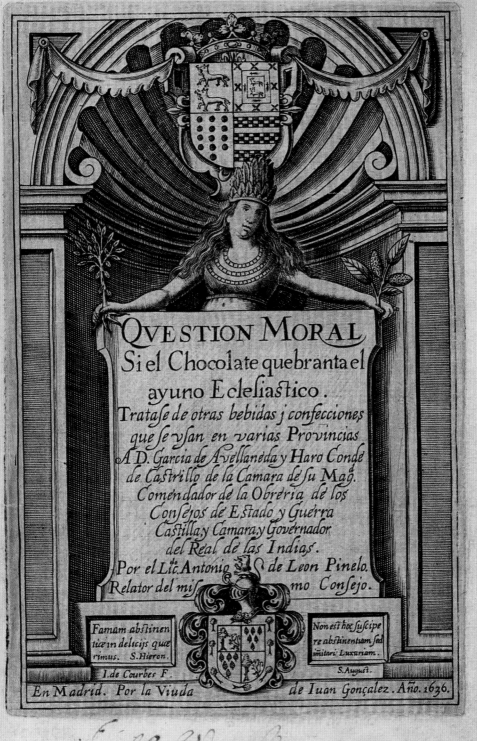

QVESTION MORAL
Si el Chocolate quebranta el
ayuno Ecleſiaſtico.
Trataſe de otras bebidas j confecciones,
que ſe yſan en varias Provincias
A D. Garcia de Avellaneda y Haro Conde
de Caſtrillo de la Camara de ſu Mag.
Comendador de la Obreria de los
Conſejos de Eſtado y Guerra
Caſtilla, y Camara, y Governador.
del Real de las Indias.
Por el Lic. Antonio de Leon Pinelo.
Relator del miſmo Conſejo.

Famam abſtinen
tiæ in delicijs quæ
rimus. S. Hieron.

Non eſt hoc ſuſcipe
re abſtinentiam ſed
imitari Luxuriam.
S. Auguſt.

I. de Courbes F.

En Madrid. Por la Viuda   de Iuan Gonçalez. Año. 1636.

On the other hand, Dominican monks, who believed in a more orthodox doctrine, were against the consumption of chocolate during the ecclesiastical fasting. The question originated from a doctor in Seville, who, in 1591, published his first book: *Problemas y Secretos Maravillosos de las Indias*: he claimed that cocoa also contained butter, which gave substance and could make you fat and "this alone is enough to make chocolate a cause of breaking the fasting." According to this point of view, those who drank chocolate during fasting were sinners. A few years later a Jesuit theologian, father Antonio Escobar y Mendoza replied to this question: he wrote that the use of the beverage made from cocoa was allowed as long as water was used instead of milk to melt the seeds.

The question was so serious that even several Popes spoke about it, starting from Pius V, the pontiff who had won the Battle of Lepanto. He too had been enchanted by the drink, after having tasted it in 1569. The pontiff decided that the drink did not break the fasting just as long as it was prepared with water. Others to take an interest in the issue were, Clement VII Aldobrandini, Urban VIII, Clement IX and Pope Lambertini, and lastly Benedict XIV from Bologna.

To solve the vexing question, Cardinal Francesco Maria Brancaccio's book came on the scene, *De chocolatis potu diatribe*: in this work the cardinal claimed that hot chocolate was a drink *per accidens*, but after all it was still a liquid. So, it was permitted during ecclesiastical fasting because *liquida non frangunt jejunum* ("drinks don't interrupt the fasting").

CHOCOLATE IN ART

The success of chocolate among the European aristocracy consolidated definitely in the 1700s, which became the "golden age" of this product in all the capitals, from Turin to Paris, from London to Vienna. During that time, before the ending of the *Ancien Régime*, chocolate inspired many artists who depicted it in paintings, described it in poems and musical works. The famous painting by Pietro Longhi (1701-1785), *La cioccolata del mattino* ("The Morning Chocolate") is an example of this. It depicts a servant handing the chocolate pot to the noble lady of the house, while she is surrounded by friends. A languid and seductive atmosphere which was described both by Giuseppe Parini (1729-1799) in his poem *Il giorno* and by playwright Carlo Goldoni (1707-1793) in his playful drama *The Conversation*, in which the great Venetian author's love for steaming hot cups reaches its peak: "What a

43 - The painting "The Morning Chocolate" by Venetian Pietro Longhi (1775/1780).

delicate drink! / What a pleasure it gives me! / And so goes the chocolate / Which gives taste and health." Wolfgang Amadeus Mozart (1756-1791) repeated these words in his opera *Così fan tutte*: in a scene from the first act, the soprano voice, the little servant Despina prepares breakfast for her mistress: "What a wretched life / A lady's maid leads! [...] I've been beating this for half an hour / And now the chocolate's ready; yet though my tongue's / Hanging out, must I just stand and smell it?" The most iconic picture, also picked up by the American confectionary industry at the beginning of the 1800s, remains *Das Schokoladenmädchen* ("The Chocolate Lady"): it was drawn in crayons by the Swiss artist Jean-Étienne Liotard in 1745, during his stay in the Hapsburg court of Maria Theresa, and it is now kept in the Old Masters Gallery in Dresden. The details are painted with vivid precision: on the shiny lacquered tray there's a *trembleuse* cup with a "mancerina" to hold it and near that a glass of water which gives us the idea of a refined breakfast ritual. A small glimpse of domestic life, in which the ritual of hot chocolate in the morning has a significant role.

44 - "The Chocolate Lady" by Swiss painter Jean-Étienne Liotard (1745).

45 - "A Holstein Peasant Woman" (German region of Hamburg) by painter Fritz Westphal (1867).

THE DUTCH AND ENGLISH REVOLUTION

The breakthrough in the history of chocolate only came at the beginning of the 1800s, in Amsterdam, the center of European cocoa trade. The main responsible of the so called "Dutch revolution" was the chemist Coenraad J. van Houten, who in 1828, opened a chocolate factory with his father Casparus. In the small laboratory, the two craftsmen were able to build a hydraulic press that could reduce the cocoa beans into dust with alkaline salts – a bath of magnesium, calcium and potassium. Thanks to this process that was later named *Dutching*, they were able to extract the fat part of the seeds which makes up about 50% of it, making cocoa butter for the first time. It was the invention needed to allow the Food of the Gods to go from a liquid form to a solid one: by adding the butter to the mass of toasted beans a solid bar could be created, that melted at human body temperature.

Confectionery industries involved in the processing of cocoa flourished during the 1800s. In England, a group of Quaker pharmacists (a protestant religious movement with very strict Calvinist rules, especially opposed to alcohol) belonging to the Fry dynasty, in Bristol, gave a moral stamp to chocolate production, as an alternative to beer and whisky. After the founder Joseph Storrs Fry, it was Francis Jr who invented the first chocolate bar which could really be "eaten."

46 - An advertising postcard by the English company Fry (1912).

47 - A advertising poster of Fry's Cocoa Powder (1906).

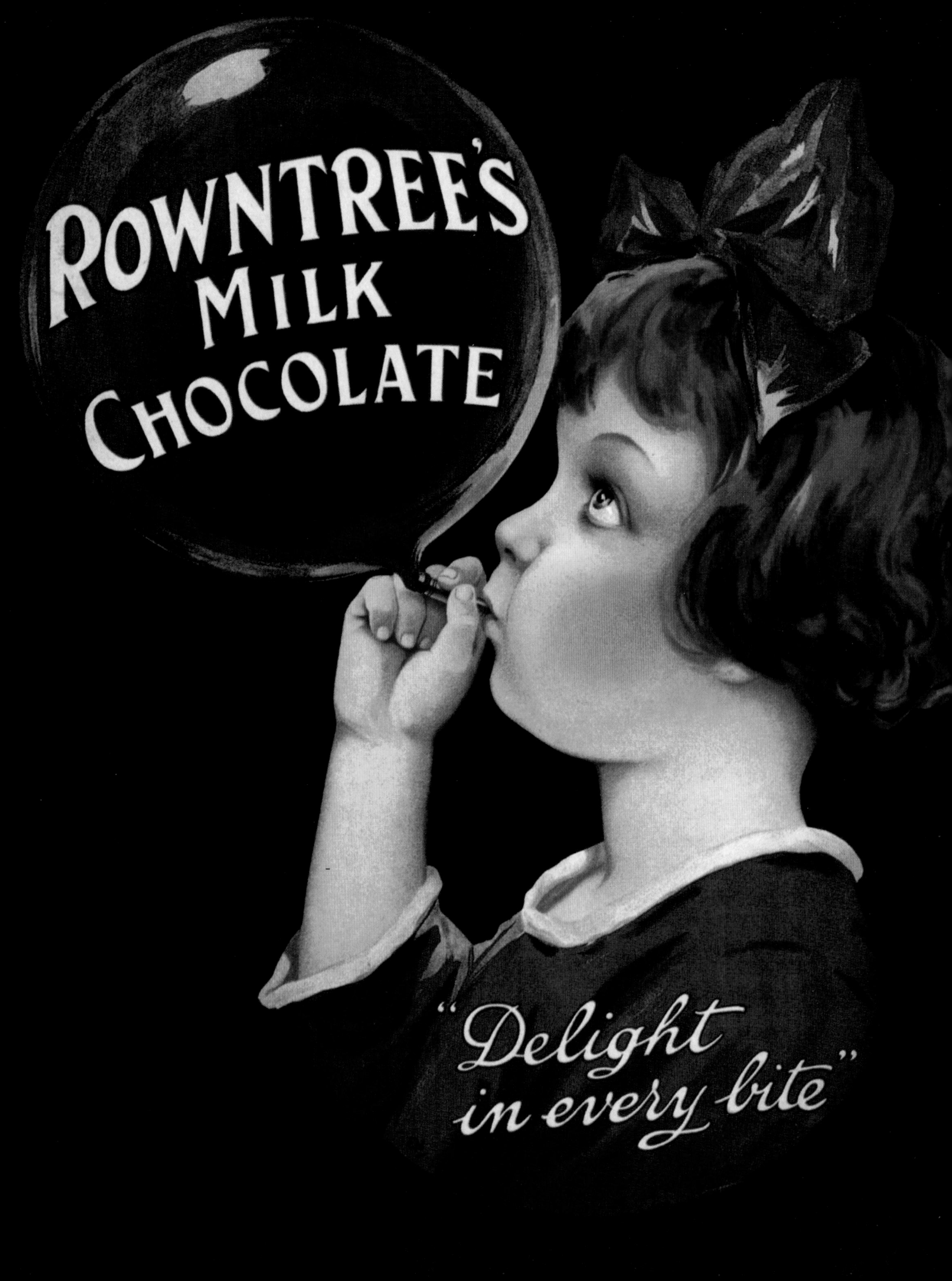
ROWNTREE'S
MILK
CHOCOLATE
"Delight
in every bite"

49 - A postcard of English company Cadbury (1889) to advertise the consumption of hot chocolate even in summer.

It was a huge success and the company became the official supplier of the Royal Navy, to which half of the production was destined. After the First World War, the company merged with the competitor company Cadbury Brothers from Birmingham, founded by another Quaker. To this day, it is still one of the most important confectionary brands in the world. Along with these two pioneers came also Rowntree of York, another family belonging to the same religious belief: it was a confectionary brand that stayed at the top until 1988, when it was bought by the Swiss company Nestlé.

Meanwhile in France other machines were being experimented, like the *melangeur*, a mill similar to the one which is still used for the handmade production of olive oil. It was made of two big granite rollers which turned on a plate made of the same material, it was used to crush and blend cocoa with sugar, at increasing temperatures and it took the place of many men who before were needed to use the *metate*, a concave stone heated by a flame, which was invented in Mexico. The Frenchman François Pellettier stood out in this activity, as he managed to produce up to a hundred kilograms a day using a 4-horsepower steam blender. Laboratories soon all acquired steam machines, in Paris and mainly in Bayonne, a small town on the border with Spain which based its economy mainly on the processing of the *Theobroma cacao*.

48 - A poster of English company Rowntree, promoting milk chocolate among children, "delight in every bite."

NAPOLEON, GIANDUIA AND SWITZERLAND

After defeating the British in the naval battle of Trafalgar, Napoleon went back to his expansion in Europe by defeating the Prussians: hence in November 1806 he arrived in Berlin, were he applied the so-called Continental System, which denied any commercial or naval contact with the British islands. The result was immediate: colonial merchandise such as cocoa and sugar, became expensive and hard to find. The French and Germans overcame that by extracting sugar from beetroot, while chocolate makers in Turin – who supplied the whole of Europe with their subalpine delights – were forced to create a chocolate surrogate following the recipe from a

50 - An advertisement of the late 19th century of Caffarel Prochet: the chocolatiers who created the gianduiotto.

little book written by encyclopedia writer Antonio Bazzarino, who gave his book a significant title, which was *Theorical-practical Plan of National Chocolate Replacement*.

In his volume, the author suggested substituting the expensive cocoa with almonds, lupines and "the occidental hazelnut" easily available on the hills of Langhe and Monferrato, a few kilometers away from Turin, the Savoy capital. And so, two craftsmen, Prochet & Caffarel, made a surrogate which consisted of one third of hazelnuts, one third of cocoa paste and one third of sugar. It was the famous Gianduiotto, with its typical upside-down boat shape. It was the first wrapped chocolate in the world and it was named after the carnival character from Turin, Gianduia: the year was 1867.

51 - 19th century advertising poster of Moriondo & Gariglio, founded in Turin in 1869.

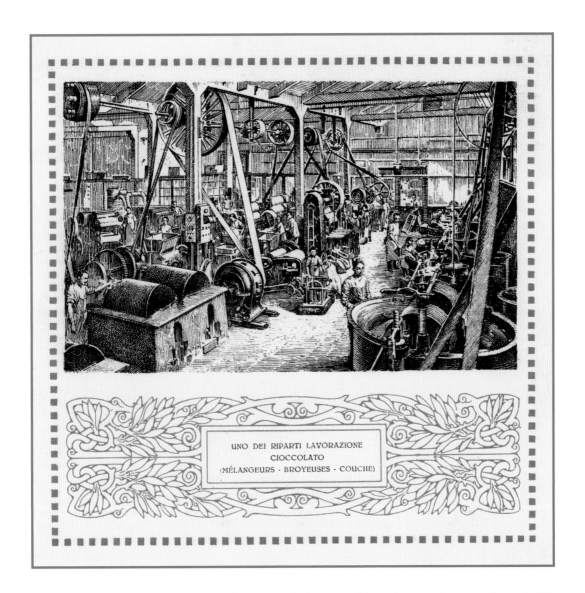

UNO DEI RIPARTI LAVORAZIONE
CIOCCOLATO
(MÉLANGEURS - BROYEUSES - COUCHE)

53 - A cocoa processing department of Venchi in Turin at the beginning of the 20th century (corporate album of 1927).

By then, Turin was the traditional capital of homemade chocolate in Southern Europe. Many famous brands saw the light in those years, like the laboratory of Silviano Venchi, opened in 1878 and, even before that Caffarel in 1826, Talmone in 1850 and Pastiglie Leone in 1857. At the beginning of the 1900s the Piedmontese businessman Riccardo Gualino reunited many confectionary industries in the brand Unica ("National Unity of Chocolate and Associates"), starting the production with three thousand employees, in a big factory in Turin. His aim was to spread the Food of the Gods among the people, in direct competition with Buitoni Perugina, who on the other hand had a more restricted type of production. In 1934, Gualino turned his business into Venchi-Unica, merging two companies. He stayed in the business until the 1970s. After many ups and downs in the business, Venchi has recently been revived by Italian businessmen, while Caffarel is now part of the Lindt Swiss group.

52 - The famous advertisement of Talmone: the Due Vecchi *("Two Old People") designed by Roberto Ochser (1890).*

54 - Advertising poster designed by Leonetto Cappiello for Turin-based Venchi (circa 1921).

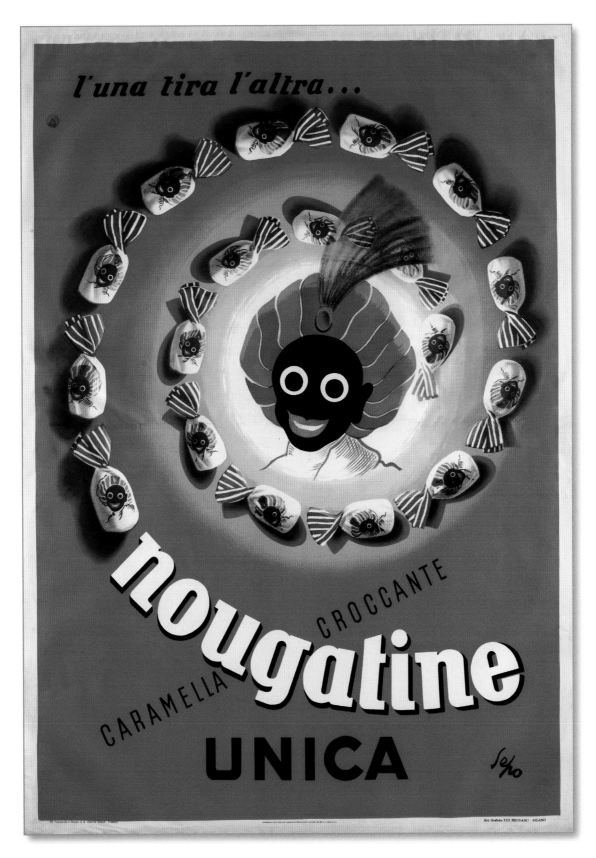

55 - The artist Severo Pozzati signed this poster for Unica with his initials Sepo (between 1924 and 1934).

56 - A popular poster of the Swiss Cailler, from the 1930s.

During this pioneering age, many eager young people came down from the Swiss canton of Ticino and from the Grisons to the Piedmontese capital, driven by the desire to learn a craft and make a living.

Among them there was almost surely François Louis Callier, who in 1819 founded the first Swiss chocolate factory in Corsier, near Vevey, where he sold his vanilla and cinnamon chocolates. Then his company was taken over by Nestlé, which today is the biggest food industry in the world, and still has its headquarters on the banks of Lake Geneva.

The Swiss were among the last pioneers to reach the Food of the Gods, but they

57 - Swiss Nestlé advertisement dedicated to children, from the 1930s.

gave a big boost to the development of the industry, with two inventions for which all *chocoholics* – term used to define chocolate lovers who are almost "addicted" to it – are eternally grateful. The first is milk chocolate, made by Daniel Peter in 1875, who was able to use the invention of a milk formula by chemist Henri Nestlé. The second is dark chocolate, which was "invented" between 1879 and 1880 by Rudolph Lindt. Lindt had forgotten to turn off a machine and thanks to this he was able to perfection the heated conching process by adding cocoa butter, thanks to which all the flavors of the chocolate bar are enhanced.

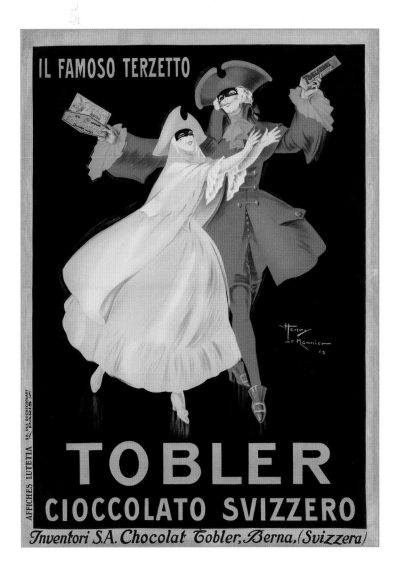

The innovations were over, now it was time for the big industries to take over. David Sprügli aquired Lindt in 1890 and today Lindt & Sprügli is one of the biggest confectionary brands in the world. The first Swiss bars, pastilles and "diablotin" are attributed to Philipp Suchard, in 1825. Later on in 1901 he launched the Milka milk chocolate bar: the brand was then absorbed by the Kraft Food industry which became Mondelēz International in 2012 (with its headquarters in the United States, near Chicago). Toblerone, the famous filled bar invented in Berna in 1900 by Theodore Tobler, is also a part of this group, and its name is a combination of the name of its inventor and the Italian word *torrone*.

58 - Leonetto Cappiello signed this poster, where children are again protagonists, for the Swiss Suchard (1925).

59 - A Tobler advertisement (1923), designed by Henry Le Monnier, poster artist from Paris.

60-61 - Artist Johann Georg van Caspel signs the poster (1897) for the Dutch company Karstel.

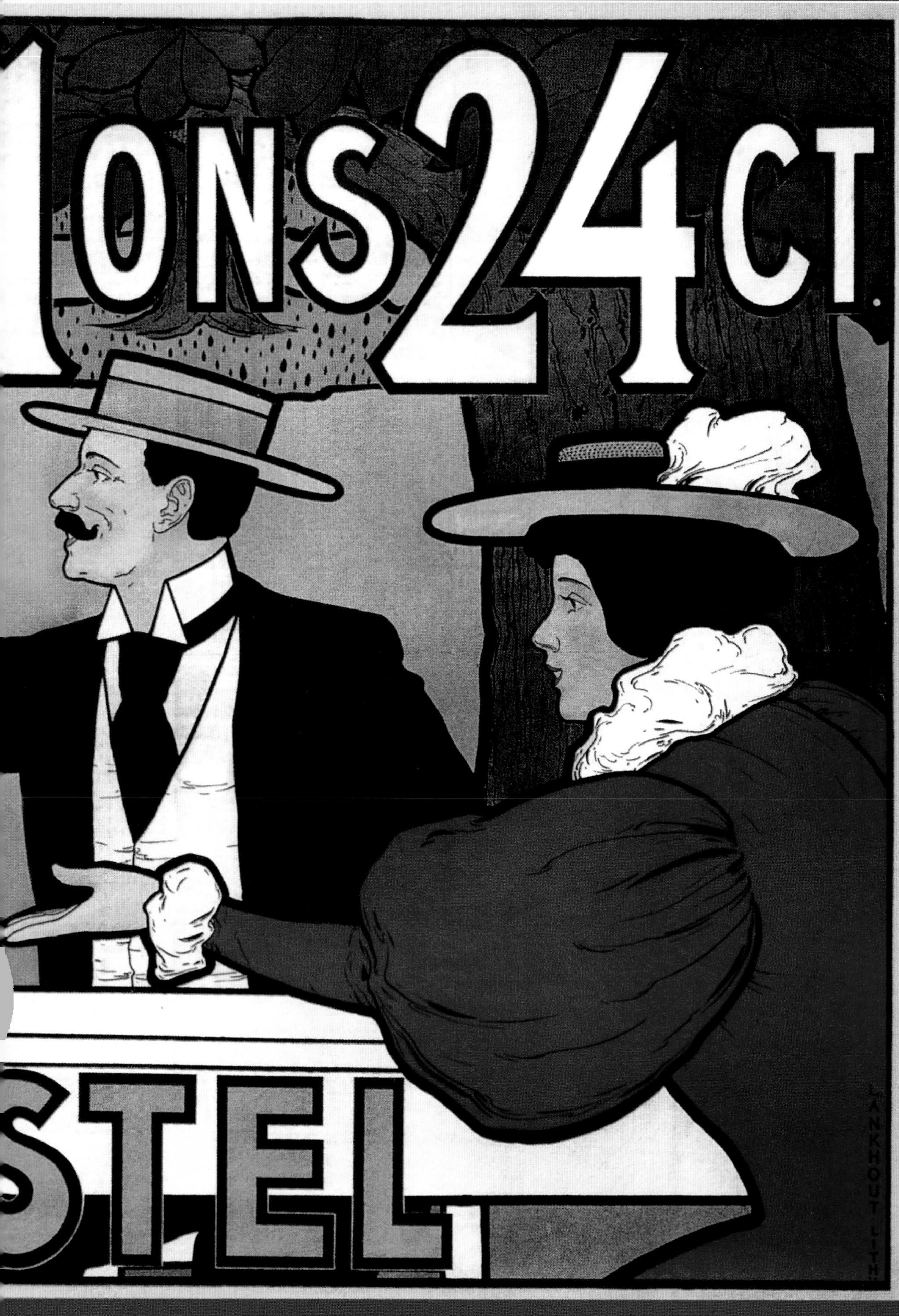
ONS 24 CT.
STEL
LANKHOUT LITH.

THE BIG CHOCOLATE COMPANIES

Hershey, Pennsylvania is maybe the sweetest city on earth. Here everything is dedicated to chocolate: the museum on the corner of Chocolate Avenue and Cocoa Avenue recreates the Willy Wonka chocolate factory's atmosphere, as described in the novel by Roald Dahl and the movie by Tim Burton. The streetlights are shaped like the most famous American chocolate, the Kiss. The city takes its name from Milton Hershey, a candy maker from Philadelphia who in 1893 realized he had to change his job: "Candies are just a trend, chocolate is going to stay." This businessman is considered the father of American chocolate in the United States: he won over the consumers with his famous Kiss, the chocolate launched in 1907, a flat-bottomed drop wrapped in aluminum paper with a little paper crest at the top. Mister Hershy is also known for his philanthropy: he was the one to build the city's hospital, the school, the bank, the library, the playground and up until now the charity who owns two thirds of the actions, the Milton Hershey School Trust has always refused proposals from the biggest multinational confectionary companies of the world. The ranking based on the world market's share, made by Nielsen, places Hershey's in fourth place in the big top ten of world chocolates after Mars, Mondelēz and Ferrero.

The American company Mars has a place at the top of the big chocolate companies: it is based in Mclean, Virginia, and, after four generations, it is still owned by the family of the founder, Clarence Mars, who opened a candy factory in 1911. It was then converted to a chocolate factory with the arrival of the Milky Way, invented in 1923. Mars bars were invented by the English section of the company in 1932, with its typical malt and caramel taste. The company is one of the most reserved in the world, the family does not give interviews and no visits are allowed inside the factories.

The Ferrero group has the same way of thinking. The company was founded in 1946 in Alba, in the south of Piedmont, by baker Pietro Ferrero: he was able to transform his small artisan laboratory into an industry thanks to a surrogate made with hazelnuts, cocoa, sugar and vegetable fats called the Giandujot. In 1949 it became a spread (Supercream) and finally it was called Nutella in 1964 by his son Michele Ferrero. A new type of chocolate product was born, besides bars and chocolates, i.e. chocolate spreads. Today, the Italian company is a multinational based in Luxemburg, with 23 factories in the five continents which make Kinder eggs and the Rocher, a product of the artisan chocolate tradition which is now listed as the most sold chocolate in the world.

Thanks to these big industries chocolate is now a mass-produced product, distributed in every continent. But in the last few years there has been a new attention from gourmets for a high-quality Food of the Gods, made in small quantities, to be tasted with the same care that a sommelier has towards a good wine.

63 - American company Mars is the largest chocolate maker in the world: here, an advertisement from the 1950s.

64-65 - A poster of American company Hershey dedicated to the Kiss chocolate, created in 1911.

Smart
set-up

MARS CHOCOLATE Toasted Almond BAR

Chocolate from the finest imported chocolate beans

  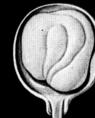

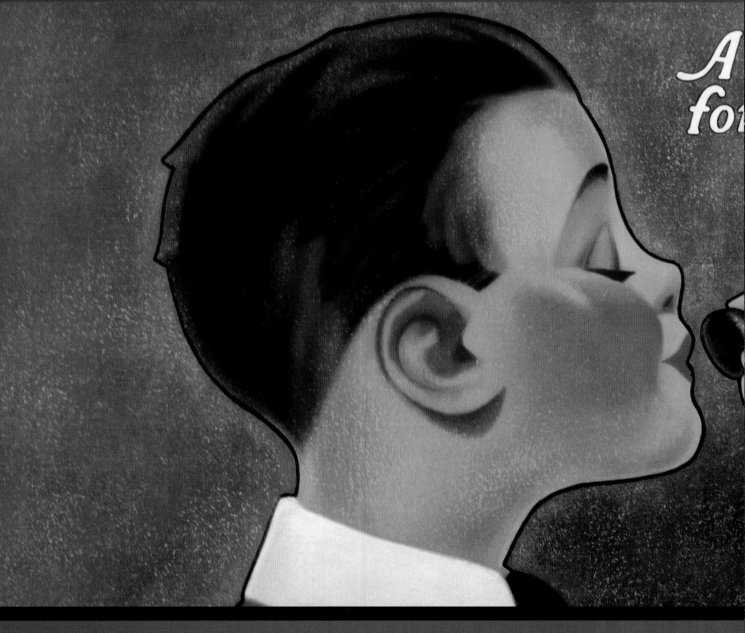

THE WORLD
OF COCOA

The world of cocoa can be divided in two parts: the equatorial belt, where the cocoa plant is cultivated, and the Northern hemisphere, whose inhabitants eat the chocolate produced from the cocoa beans. This tropical plant has ancient origins, and it is cultivated only in the hottest, most humid areas of the Earth, in countries that rarely process the fruits, where the farmers who cultivate the plant have probably never even tasted a bar of chocolate. On the other hand, Europe, Russia and the United States – and recently even China and India – buy, process and consume ever increasing amounts of the Food of the Gods.

The growth of the world cocoa production has been very fast: according to data from Icco, the International Cocoa Organization, before 1830, when the large chocolate factories of the industrialized world entered into operation, only 10,000 tons of beans were harvested throughout the planet. Nowadays, on average the global crop is estimated at around 4.5 million tons per year, with variations according to the climatic conditions: global warming is considered a danger to the plant, which needs humidity.

In recent years, the price per tonne has fluctuated between 2000 and 3000 euros: about 2-3 euros per kg, but sometimes, for the less valuable cocoa it can even drop to under 1 euro, and there are consistent differences, based on the quality and country of origin. The artisan chocolate makers that look for the *grand cru* can pay up to 6-8 euro for a kilo (2 lbs) of beans, buying them directly from the producer, with whom they come to a supply agreement, so they can follow all the production stages. This explains why the price of a bar of dark chocolate can vary greatly.

Is it really necessary for a "Chocolate sommelier," to know something about the plant he uses in his products, about its *cultivar* and its country of origin? The answer is: yes. And the comparison with the world of wine production can help us understand. Just as the connoisseur seeks to know the *terroir* from which the wine is being tasted, is interested in the grape variety with which it has been vinified, knows a particular hill and wants to understand the exposure of the vineyard, in the same way, it is important to know where the cocoa comes from, more than knowing the percentage of cocoa contained in a bar. The current trend, in fact, is to produce "mono-origin" fondant bars, that is, made with cocoa from the same country, or even from the same plantation.

67 - A figure by German naturalist Maria Sibylla Merian (1647-1717) illustrating the cocoa fruit.

P. Sluyter Sculp.

68 - A plantation in Cameroon, one of the leading African cocoa-producing countries.

It isn't really a case of fashion, but in a way, it is a return to the origins. This search for the quality of the raw materials allows the consumer to compare between different productions, as is normally done for wine. With regard to chocolate, the percentage of cocoa is certainly not indifferent: for a good dark chocolate it is better to choose a quantity exceeding 65%. This does not mean, however, that a higher percentage, around 80 or 85%, gives it a better taste. It's a bit like wine: a Sicilian or Argentinian red that develops 15 degrees alcohol is certainly no better than an elegant burgundy or an aristocratic Barolo, which stops at 13 or 13.5 degrees.

According to FAO (the UN Food and Agriculture Organisation), there are between four and five million farmers in the world devoting themselves to chocolate cultivation, mostly in small plantations, with an economy that gives a living to 40-50 million people. The plantation farmer's earnings, unfortunately, are rather low, compared to the added value that is given to the dazzling storefront window of an important patisserie in one of the great capitals of the world. This is because cocoa, in third place in world trade after sugar and coffee, is a *soft commodity*: in the economic language this is the definition of raw materials which can be easily stored, such as food (wheat, maize), or metals and minerals (*hard commodities* being gold, silver, petroleum).

The price of the beans is negotiated in the commodity exchanges: for cocoa, trading takes place in New York, usually through ICE (International Exchange) and in London at the Liffe (London International Financial Futures and Options Exchange), using *futures*, i.e. term contracts in which the person subscribing the title undertakes to purchase the product at maturity. Unfortunately, this method reduces cocoa to a merchandise in which the quality has a low relevance, while the financial mechanisms typical of the stock market prevail. So, the farmer who meticulously takes care of his crop, personally deals with the fermentation and drying of the seeds, discards the flawed beans, receives from the middlemen – in South America they are called *Coyotes* – the same price as those who don't take as much care and just mix all the beans together without worrying about the quality.

CHOCOLATE SOMMELIER

69 - The cabosse *(pods) are the fruits that grow directly on the trunk of the cocoa plant.*

In recent years, however, both industries producing *premium* products and the most careful artisans have begun to establish direct relations between plantations and their laboratories: the cocoa culture has grown a lot. And that's why chocolate enthusiasts can also benefit from greater knowledge of this plant, which is an extraordinary example of biodiversity.

THANKS TO THE GNATS

Walking through a "chocolate forest" is an intense emotion, each tree produces one to two kilograms of beans ready to be processed. The beans are contained in the fruits, from ten to twenty for each plant, they have the shape of small colored footballs, attached directly to the trunk – a type of growth that in botany is defined as cauliflory.

From each tree only four, 3.5 oz (100 g) bars can be obtained, at the most. With a cost that varies between two to six euros for 2 lbs (1 kg) of dried beans, the value of chocolate oscillates between 5/6 euros (for dark chocolate containing 50% cocoa, on the mass market) and 20/30 euros (for a high-quality artisan *grand cru* dark chocolate containing 75% cocoa).

It is actually quite difficult to visit a cocoa plantation, they are located only in the equatorial belt of the planet, between the 20th parallel north and the 20th to the south, at an altitude of less than 500 meters above sea level, with some exceptions, according to the climate, in the highlands of Cameroon, Uganda, Colombia. The cocoa tree is rather delicate and fragile, because it does not withstand temperatures below 61 °F (16 °C) and it needs a lot of humidity, at least 75%, with a dry season of not more than three months and many rains. The tree is also prone to pest attacks. Since the pollination of the flowers (only one in a thousand will give the fruit) is done through insects, *Diptera* or mini-flies, it is preferable to cultivate it in the shade of "mother plants," like banana trees and coconut palms.

In its wild state, *Theobroma cacao* can reach over 60 feet (20 m) high; when it is cultivated, however, it is kept under 15 feet (5 m). It becomes productive after four or five years and reaches its maximum yield after around twenty years, to live until forty.

It is an evergreen, with alternating leaves of oblong oval shape, slightly wavy, about 8 in (20 cm) long. Each plant develops up to a thousand small flowers, which last for only two days and the fruit, thanks to the work of the gnats, will mature in four or five months.

The Spaniards christened the fruits *cabosse* or *cabosside* (in English "cocoa pod"), which they said resembled the heads of the natives: they weigh from 7 oz (200 g) up to 2 lbs (1 kg), and once detached from the tree with a machete and split in half, they offer their precious treasure. They contain from 30 to 40 seeds, of light color, as large as almonds, wrapped in a whitish sugary mucilage. Once separated from this substance, the seeds will begin their fermentation process. In some countries, as in Peru and Brazil, the liquid that is collected from the separation is used as a drink or turned into liquor.

From a botanical point of view, the cocoa plant is a true enigma. There are many species and their classification has been surrounded by controversy for years. According to the most recent genetic studies, it has been classified as a *Malvacae* – the same family as mallow, cotton, roselle – while it had previously been inserted among the *Sterculiaceae* (cola nut). The origin, as we have seen, was identified in the Amazon rainforest, in the present-day Brazil.

NOT JUST THREE VARIETIES

Everything gets even more complicated when having to identify the subspecies of *Theobroma*, which are roughly twenty. Among the best known and exploited is the *Theobroma bicolor*, from which the "pataste" comes from, very similar to the cocoa, from whose fruits the Mayans probably produced the first chocolate: in Brazil it is called "mocambo." In Colombia, Peru and Brazil – in the rainforest – a fruit is collected, called *cupuaçu*. It is born from *Theobroma grandiflorum* and it has a mixed flavor of pineapple and banana, with hints of cocoa.

As for the "varieties" of *Theobroma cacao*, until a few years ago, three were traditionally identified: Criollo, Forastero and Trinitario. To simplify our analysis, we will begin with this classification. There are, however, others, either related to the germplasm or the shape, or according to the commercial classification determined by the Icco.

71 - A cabosse just split open reveals the cocoa beans still wrapped in a white mucilage.

Then the fermentation begins, which is a process similar to that of grapes when they turn into wine. The fava beans, still raw and dripping with their mucilaginous pulp, are placed in large bins and covered with banana leaves (in small family plantations) or under special canopies. The fermentation process, in which the precursors of cocoa aromas develop, must be checked and meticulously followed. Thus, the heat is generated (around 104/122 °F or 40/50 °C) with which the sugar pulp liquefies – which must be turned often – allowing the tannin of the seeds to oxidise, which gives the typical brown color. The duration of this phase varies according to the quality, usually for the Forastero it is longer, from five days to a week, while for the aromatic cocoa it stops at three days.

Finally, it is necessary to proceed with the drying: this happens in the sun if the climatic conditions allow it, or in special hot air ovens. Even this phase is decisive, as it stops the fermentation process, prevents the onset of mold, limits the acidity that, in case it is excessive, constitutes a serious flaw of the chocolate. It takes from one to two weeks, so that the moisture content of the beans is reduced to about 7 and 8%.

At this point the cocoa is ready for its magical transformation into the Food of the Gods, a process that usually takes place away from the plantations. The beans are placed in 110/170 lbs (50/70 kg) jute bags, which must be stored in suitable environments, with good air circulation and sheltered from the sun and weather.

78 - The drying of cocoa beans takes place on a plantation and must be inspected.

SUSTAINABILITY CONDITIONS

The demand for raw material to produce the many chocolate specialities is growing, as well as the production of cocoa seeds, especially in West Africa. While the value chain generated to reach the finished product is around 120 billion dollars, only 9 billion of these profits go to the primary sector, the plantations, while 28 billion represent the value of the raw products (the cocoa paste) and as much as 87 for sweets, snacks, pralines and bars. The volatility of the world cocoa market puts small farmers at risk, even if the two African countries that produce 60% of the total, Ivory Coast and Ghana, have studied different price control mechanisms with guaranteed quotations.

Globally, it is estimated that about 5% of the world harvest of *Theobroma cacao* is made in Africa, followed by Central and South America with 17% (Brazil and Ecuador are the major producers) and from Asia and Oceania with 7% (Indonesia and Papua New Guinea).

Cocoa is a key resource for many developing countries, although it is cultivated mainly in small, family-run businesses. According to research from the University of New Orleans, United States, in Africa at least two million children are involved in the production of the Food of the Gods. Since the beginning of the century a lot has been done to create a greater sustainability for the whole chain. The birth of the World Cocoa Foundation, which now has more than one hundred members, including almost all the major processing industries, which aims to create a cocoa production "in which farmers thrive, cocoa communities can grow, human rights are respected and the environment is preserved."

There is therefore a hope: that "bitter chocolate," the one that deforests and exploits minors, can be stopped. For many years now, fair trade certifications have been launched – equal and responsible trade, which, however, does not always produce high quality chocolate – or environmental organizations, such as the Rainforest Alliance, which has now reached with its reassuring brand logo – a cute frog – a rather substantial production, for a total of more than one million hectares cultivated, equal to about 13% of the total.

Climate change is also negatively affecting cocoa cultivation: higher temperatures, unpredictable rainfall and a shift in growing seasons are worrying phenomena. Some large multinationals are studying genetic modifications to protect the cocoa, but the entry of GMOs into this chain – which so far was immune to them – could endanger biodiversity. The environmental organizations are convinced that it is possible to invest mainly in training, to achieve efficient and sustainable agricultural management, to stop the destructive cycle of poverty and deforestation.

80-81 - Jute sacks with dried cocoa beans from the São Tomé and Principe archipelago.

THE SECRETS
OF PROCESSING

If you are a chocolate enthusiast and really want to know all its secrets, then we suggest you pay a visit to a laboratory in which the beans are transformed into delicious dark or milk chocolate. While it is true that the harvesting and processing of cocoa is rather complex, the alchemical transformation from the bean to the bar is even longer and requires very delicate phases. The intoxicating aromas that can be breathed in a *Chocolate Factory*, like that of Willy Wonka, immortalized in Dahl's novel, are incomparable. The image of brown gold waves and the pipes that took it to the various working stations has remained in the collective memory, as evidenced by the words of the famous novel: "in that river there is enough chocolate to fill every bathtub in the entire country! And all the swimming pools as well. Isn't it terrific? And just look at my pipes! They suck up the chocolate and carry it away to all the other rooms in the factory where it is needed! Thousands of gallons an hour..."

In fact, visiting one of the companies that produce the Food of the Gods, starting with those beans arriving in sacks from distant countries, isn't so easy. Very often pralines, mini-bars, *dragées* or truffles are made using "cocoa mass," or "cocoa liquor," a semi-finished product that is supplied to artisan laboratories by large companies specializing in cocoa processing, such as Barry Callebaut – A French-Belgian multinational company headquartered in Zürich, which alone moves 1.7 million tons of cocoa, one third of the world's harvest – or the French Valrhona, which caters mainly to professionals.

In recent years, however, there has been an increase of the artisans who passionately take care of the entire production chain, and also many quality industries now process the raw materials coming from the producing countries.

Let's take a look then at all the traditional phases of the transformation of cocoa into chocolate, with the warning that the processes can also be very different depending on the type of producer – large company or small artisan – and the result that they want to obtain. Moreover, for some years now, *raw chocolate* has become very fashionable, according to the dictates of rawists and vegans. It is made by avoiding to "bake" the beans above 107 °F (42 °C). It is a particular production process. We will talk about it, but for many reasons – not least the sanitary one – we think it is a way of processing the cocoa that does not exalt all its characteristics and aromas.

MASS, POWDER AND BUTTER

Sacks with dried cocoa beans are loaded on ships and, after a long journey, from one of the producing countries they arrive in the processing plants, usually very far from the plantations. In recent years, many projects have been created to start up production plants on site, both in West Africa and in many Latin American countries, so as to try and keep the added value where the fruit is cultivated, but this process is still only at a beginning phase.

The first step is the transformation of the dried seeds into three types of semi-finished goods: the cocoa mass (or "paste" or "liquor"), cocoa powder and cocoa butter.

The cocoa mass is obtained from the mixture and refining of the beans, after roasting, and is the basis of all chocolate productions. When a label states that a bar is 70%, it means that it was made with 70 grams of this "pure cocoa liquor," with the addition of 30 grams of sugar.

Cocoa butter and powder (the one used to dust the cappuccino or tiramisu) can be obtained with another type of processing – by squeezing the toasted beans with large industrial presses. Cocoa butter is the fat naturally contained in the seeds: after the squeezing, filtering and purifying processes, it can be solidified and takes on the appearance of a slab of butter.

84-85 - The toasted beans from which the cocoa mass, the cocoa butter and the cocoa powder are made.

It is a noble and costly fatty matter, which is used for cosmetic purposes (for example, as lip balm) or added to the cocoa paste to give more brilliance and malleability to the chocolate (especially in Easter eggs and in large bars used by professionals for "coating"). Its processing results in a solid "slab" of cocoa butter, which still contains 10-20% of fat: from this, the cocoa powder is obtained.

Before starting any process, it is necessary to check the raw cocoa arriving from the plantations: there are special aspirators and magnets that can clean the contents of the sacks from unwanted material, such as stones, pieces of metal, leaves. The process can also be done by hand, where the beans are cleaned with sieves and brushes.

ROASTING

This phase is one of the most delicate in the processing of cocoa. The beans are brought to temperatures which vary between 230-356 °F (110-180 °C), with a time that goes from a minimum of 15/20 minutes up to one hour. The objective of roasting or toasting is to develop all the aromas; therefore, such process must not be too short, because the cocoa would have herbaceous and acidic notes, nor too long, because excessive exposure to heat could burn all the aromas. It is a process very similar to that of coffee roasting, and actually, some old artisan machines can be used for both raw materials. These are the toasters, equipped with the classic horizontal wheel to let the seeds cool down. But the industry today uses hot-air tunnels for this process along with more sophisticated technologies. Today, the roasting has been speeded up, after a "breath" of steam that kills the microbes: which used to be done at 266 °F (130 °C), but now is around 230 °F (110 °C).

HUSKS REMOVAL

Having lost much of its moisture, the *cascara* that wraps the seed, that is the husk, can be detached more easily and generally this operation is done after roasting. The machine also breaks the cocoa into small pieces, called nibs (in French *grué*) and with blasts of air completely eliminates the external husk.

MILLING

It is the last phase, which transforms the grain into cocoa mass, and is also called crushing. The more traditional machining involves a circular tank with two large granite wheels, called *melangeur*. The heat and the rubbing action melt at around 140-158 °F (60-70 °C) the fatty matter, giving life to a fragrant and dense brown liquid, that once cooled can be formed into large "slabs" of semi-finished product, ready, after other passages, to be turned into the Food of the Gods.

87 - In some countries artisan methods are still used to toast the cocoa beans.

HOW A CHOCOLATE BAR IS BORN

From this moment on we enter the magical world of Vianne Rocher, the protagonist of *Chocolat*, the novel by Joanne Harris: a chocolat bar is about to be born, from the cocoa mass. "There is an endless fascination in handling the raw dullish blocks of couverture [a type of chocolate, similar to dark chocolate but with more cocoa butter, made for the professionals, A/N], in grating them by hand – I never use electric mixers – into the large ceramic pans, then melting, stirring, testing each painstaking step with the sugar thermometer until just the right amount of heat has been applied to make the change."

REFINING AND MIXING

The cocoa mass must now be refined (it used to be done with a large five-cylinder machine, a bit like a newspaper press), to reach a consistency of around 20 microns: which allows our palate to grasp all the aromas. Now it's the moment of the blending, that the chocolate pioneers always used to carry out with the stone wheeled *melangeur*. Currently, the industries and also many craftsmen employ marble mills or with large "whisks."

Other necessary ingredients are then added to the cocoa mass: for dark chocolate sugar is used, also occasionally with added vanilla, cocoa butter and a pinch of soy lecithin, a natural emulsifying agent.

In the case of milk chocolate, the cocoa mass is mixed with sugar and powdered milk. Hazelnuts are added to the gianduia, while "white chocolate" does not contain mass, but is obtained with cocoa butter, sugar, vanilla, powdered milk.

THE CONCHING

It is the process discovered only in the middle of the 19th century in Switzerland, thanks to which all the cocoa aromas are released. The name derives from the container (called *conca*) in which the mixture of cocoa mass, sugar and any other ingredients were poured, kept in a liquid state at a temperature of around 140-160 °F (60-70 °C). Traditionally, this operation was carried out with flat machines, where a roller was moved continuously back and forth, for a long time. Thanks to the temperature and the duration, two fundamental results are obtained: chocolate becomes "creamy," so it doesn't taste powdery, with annoying microgranules; and also, any excess acidity is removed. Before the introduction of this high-temperature technique, solid chocolate was not "smooth," but grainy, an example of this today is the chocolate of Modica PGI, which received European certification at the end of 2018.

Today, flat containers have almost fallen into disuse, and ball or rotating mills are used, which allow faster machining.

89 - A traditional machine for the long conching process of chocolate.

CHOCOLATE SOMMELIER

THE TEMPERING

At this point the chocolate, kept in a liquid state at a temperature of around 122 °F (50 °C), can become a bar. Before taking its final shape (a small 0.2-oz/5-gram napolitain, a block of coating chocolate, a 3.5-oz/100-gram bar, a hollow body to contain a filling, half of an Easter egg) it still has to be tempered. This operation is the last secret of the chocolatiers. Now everything happens automatically with a tempering machine, which produces an exciting and fragrant hot chocolate fountain.

Inside the machine, the temperature is gradually cooled from 122 °F to 80-82 °F (50 to 27-28 °C), with continuous mixing, and then heated to 86-87 °F (30-31 °C). This way, a perfect crystallization of the cocoa butter is obtained, and therefore a bar can be shaped in the desired way, it will be shiny and will have a homogeneous structure, able to withstand a long preservation.

The tempering can also be done in a "homemade" way, by hand. It is a process that skilled artisans used to carry out in their workshops, using a marble surface on which they stretched the mass of chocolate with a spatula, controlling the temperature. The chocolate had to be melted first at a temperature of 113-122 °F (45-50 °C), so that it deleted the memory of the crystals it had before (it does not occur at lower temperatures) and then cooled to 80-82 °F (27-28 °C). To take its final shape in a mold, it must be brought again to a temperature 86-87 °F (30-31°C). Not an easy procedure, but this is the only way to get a bar or a nice shiny praline, which breaks cleanly and "melts" in the mouth.

THE MOLDING

It is the final process, with which the chocolate is molded into the desired shape. Today, this is done with casting machines: the molds roll on a conveyor and are filled with the quantity of liquid chocolate necessary. Then, the mold is "shaken," today this is done automatically, with a kind of vibrator, but once this was also done by hand by the skilled chocolatier. Finally, the temperature must be lowered for firming: in modern plants the bar passes into a cooling tunnel. However, there are different types of plants. Apart from the simplest ones, for the production of bars, there is the one destined to making chocolate for filling, which has three "stations": one to prepare the shell, another for casting the filling and a third for the sealing. Finally, there is the processing *enrobeuse* (a French term), that is, the glazing. The glaze covers and wraps an already processed filling – that can be composed of biscuit, gianduia paste, whole hazelnuts, or the French type pralines with a *ganache* – of a thin layer of chocolate distributed by the machine.

As for the three-dimensional shapes, such as Easter eggs dolls, bunnies or Santas, etc., these are made using thick plastic molds, which can be made to rotate in a centrifuge so that the chocolate is distributed evenly on the inner wall of the mold.

91 - Ancient Easter molds: not only chocolate eggs, but also fishes and animals.

THE PACKAGING

Once the chocolate bars or specialties are ready, and come out of the cooling tunnel, they must rest before being packaged. This last phase used to be carried out by hand, usually by female staff (in 19th century pictures or in 20th century photos you can see long lines of workers equipped with gloves and caps), but now it is done by special machines. The success of a bar can also depend on a correct "wrapping," which mustn't leave any flavor on the chocolate and must preserve it correctly. In recent times, the big companies have adopted machinery that can verify, with a metal detector, the (very rare) presence of metals in the packaging intended for the consumer: a piece of metal could have detached from the wrapping machine. This is the last check before shipping the bars to the stores.

92 - For many years, chocolate bars were hand-wrapped by women: in this photograph, women working in a Venchi plant in Turin.

RAW CHOCOLATE

"Rawism" has reached even the world of chocolate and has subverted all the stages of processing that we have described so far. In fact, "raw chocolate" is a rather coarse specialty, made with a cocoa that is processed as little as possible. Its supporters theorize that in the various phases of transformation from cocoa to chocolate it should never exceed the temperature of 107 °F (42 °C), but this is rather difficult to maintain during the fermentation of the beans on the plantation, because temperatures are generally higher.

Those who produce these types of bars (often in large irregular pieces, with one hundred percent of cocoa) argue that the adopted production process maintains the healthy elements of chocolate intact – which are actually still present in every type of dark chocolate over 70% – such as antioxidants, namely polyphenols, and catechins and epicatechins. They avoid toasting the cocoa beans, which are left only to dry in the sun: this passage is emphasized in the descriptions of raw chocolate, but it must be remembered that all beans are dried before roasting. The critical point is that the bacterial charge contained in the seeds is not affected and can be very dangerous. Also, as for Modicano chocolate, the conching phase is avoided altogether.

These days many types of "raw chocolate" without refined sugar, have appeared around the world and these often also bear the vegan brand. However, there are no certifications to boast that mark on the label, to guarantee the consumer on the type of process it has undergone. This is unlike organic chocolate, which is regulated by independent control structures.

From the organoleptic point of view, rawism does not give appreciable results, because the nutrients and the functional capacities of the cocoa are only made available through the fermentation. Moreover, the roasting, albeit light, is necessary to develop the aromatic notes of cocoa. Finally, the food safety of the finished product is not guaranteed.

On their part, the producers of "raw" chocolate ensure that they have used all possible precautions, that they are supplied directly by small South American cocoa producers, and that they use crystallized coconut sugar. Sometimes they simply mix cocoa powder and cocoa butter, and in any case, they avoid any animal ingredient such as milk, do not use soy lecithin and certify their raw flakes, which are bitter and certainly not very tasty, as vegan, organic, and gluten-free.

Another process – less intransigent – is that chosen by some chocolatiers, both in Modica and Piedmont: they prefer to work chocolate at low temperatures, even after roasting, and with a short conching time. The result is a bar "rougher" than the traditional dark one, but still authentic and aromatic, in which the healthy components have remained intact.

HOW TO STORE CHOCOLATE

After packaging, manufacturers know how to store their product, usually in store rooms kept at constant temperature and low humidity.

When buying chocolate, make sure that it is stored in an air-conditioned environment without any strong lights and far from strong smelling products. High temperature, humidity and smell are the enemies of chocolate.

Jumps in temperature can cause two types of flowering: that of cocoa butter, usually for excess heat, and that of sugar, due to too much moisture. In fact, there is nothing to fear from consuming a bar that has undergone these changes, but of course it is better to avoid them.

When the Food of the Gods reaches home, what should be done to preserve it to its best? The general rule for every food is valid: consume it as soon as possible.

If you really want to keep it for longer, then there are three different types of preservation, depending on the type of chocolate:

- pralines or bars containing water, with a filling made from a cream ganache, or coated candied oranges or hazelnut creams.
- waterless bars and dry pralines.
- gianduia spreads.

In the first case, the storage temperature must be lower, around 53-57 °F (12-14 °C), with an ambient humidity of 70% and for a period not exceeding one month. In the second case it is advisable to keep it at temperatures between 60 °F to 64 °F (16 °C to 18 °C), with a relative humidity of less than 50%, in a dark environment. In the third case it can be kept in a kitchen cupboard, taking care to mix the contents of the jar before use, if the hazelnut oil has risen to the surface due to excessive heat. Also, if change in temperature has caused the sugar or cocoa butter to crystallize, it will be sufficient to heat the cream in a bain-marie to bring it back to its original state.

If you cannot store the chocolate in its original packaging, then wrap it in foil and then in cling film. Particular attention should be paid to Gianduiotti: it is better not to keep them more than three months from the date of production (even if the expiration date is generally longer) because the presence of hazelnut tends to make them rancid and oxidize this specialty.

Generally, it is better not to store chocolate in the refrigerator, also because in the presence of other foods, it will absorb their smells. When seasonal temperatures are very high, this can be an emergency solution. Still, it's better to close it in a sealed box and take it out of the fridge for a while before eating it. This operation in any case protects products rich in hazelnuts and dried fruits from rancidity and from *Plodia interpunctella*, or food moths that can attack foods based on cereals, legumes, spices if stored at temperatures above 71 °F (22 °C).

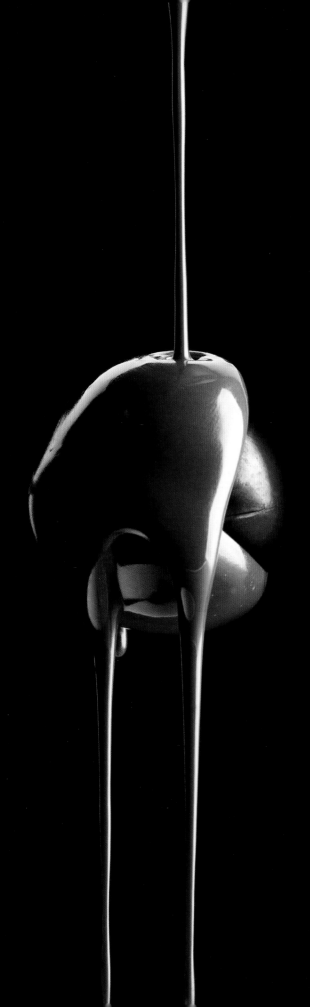

GREED IN ALL ITS FORMS

Whether it presents itself in the tempting shape of a bar, or with the appearance of a little chocolate with shiny wrapping or still as the shiny and silky icing of a Sacher-Torte, the Food of the Gods always manages to give moments of intense pleasure. It can be dark brown, almost black, or ochre, or white, or even pink in color. Its personality is always elusive.

It is a product that originates from the earth, from the fermented seeds of a fruit, but over the centuries, thanks to its ductility, man has managed to transform it into bars, pralines, Easter eggs, cakes and pastries. With the odd additions of spreads, prepared with hazelnuts as a main ingredient.

One could say that there is a kind of ambivalence to this food, an ambivalence substantiated by the reactions it has aroused over the centuries. When it is plain, dark, voluptuous, chocolate appears to be the symbol of sensuality. In its milk variation it becomes a legacy of childhood. For centuries, in its liquid state, it was called the "devil's drink," then it was turned into food, solid but always ductile, a malleable ingredient of more and more creative objects of desire.

THE CODEX POKER

It is the great "Book of Food" called *Codex Alimentarius* that has regulated world food trade since 1963 and to which almost all countries adhere.

Four types of chocolate have been recognized within this book, and they are called: dark, milk, white and gianduia. After the invention of the *ruby* version, which is pink, we could say that chocolate is a maxi poker of color with five cards.

According to the *Codex*, in order to be defined "chocolate," a food must contain at least 35% of "solid" cocoa, of which at least 18% of cocoa butter and 14% of dry non-fat cocoa.

This type of chocolate can also be called "Semi-Sweet Chocolate" (semi-bitter), or "dark."

There is also the category of coating chocolate (*couverture*), which contains more cocoa butter (at least 31%). It is used by chocolatiers for the processing of Easter eggs, hollow bodies, cakes etc.

Milk chocolate, on the other hand, must contain at least 25% of solid cocoa and between 12% and 14% of milk dry matter.

The document also lists other products that are "chocolate-based," that is: white chocolate; gianduia; gianduia with milk; "para mesa" table chocolate (also semi-bitter and bitter); vermicelli and chocolate drops (they are American products, used in biscuits and patisserie); chocolate filling (the industry produces many types of fillings, with fruit or various creams); pralines.

PRODUCT	TOTAL DRY COCOA SOLIDS	COCOA BUTTER	NON-FAT COCOA SOLIDS	TOTAL FAT	MILK FAT	MILK SOLIDS	FLOUR/ STARCH
Chocolate	≥ 35%	≥ 18%	≥ 14%				
Couverture Chocolate	≥ 35%	≥ 31%	≥ 2,5%				
Chocolate Vermicelli or Flakes	≥ 32%	≥ 12%	≥ 14%				
Milk Chocolate	≥ 25%		≥ 2,5%	≥ 25%	≥ 3,5%	≥ 14%	
Couverture Milk Chocolate	≥ 25%		≥ 2,5%	≥ 31%	≥ 3,5%	≥ 14%	
Milk Chocolate Vermicelli or Flakes	≥ 20%		≥ 2,5%	≥ 12%	≥ 3,5%	≥ 12%	
Family Milk Chocolate	≥ 20%		≥ 2,5%	≥ 25%	≥ 5%	≥ 20%	
Cream Chocolate	≥ 25%		≥ 2,5%	≥ 25%	≥ 5,5%	≥ 14%	
Skimmed Milk Chocolate	≥ 25%		≥ 2,5%	≥ 25%	≥ 1%	≥ 14%	
White Chocolate		≥ 20%				≥ 14%	
Chocolate a la taza	≥ 35%	≥ 18%	≥ 14%				≥ 8%
Chocolate familiar a la taza	≥ 30%	≥ 18%	≥ 12%				≥ 18%

LABEL ISSUES

What elements should be assessed when choosing a good chocolate? One should read the label well: it is compulsory that the percentage of cocoa mass be indicated and the commercial quality (dark, milk, white, gianduia), the place of production and the expiration date are indicated as well. Among the ingredients one can find, apart from cocoa, sugar, powdered milk and hazelnuts, also the addition of soy lecithin, vanilla and cocoa butter.

DARK OF ORIGIN

More than the percentage, it's the origin of the cocoa that counts. Nowadays, many producers add the origins to their labels, as the gourmets are looking more and more for a bitter chocolate that has a link with the territory where the cocoa was cultivated, preferring it to one obtained by mixing the fava beans from different countries (the blend method used for many years, as is the case for renown coffees and distilled spirits). A meticulous process is fundamental, for a good dark chocolate in order to experience an "upward" tasting you should start from a mass at 60% until reaching 100%, to make the most of the residual sugar left in the mouth, so as to perceive a crescendo of intensity and aroma.

Sometimes, particular areas of origin are specified on the label, like for example the Chuao, Carenero or Meridia, famous areas in Venezuela for the plantations of the rare Criollo cocoa.

If the chocolate has been produced with fava beans from one of the countries that can boast the certification of "fine" or "aromatic" cocoa, then on the label the inscription Bolivia, Costa Rica, Madagascar, Colombia, Ecuador, Peru etc. will appear, this denomination is definitely an indication of a better quality. The first dark chocolate of origin was put on the market in 1983 by the French Artisan Raymon Bonnat: to celebrate the centenary of his family business in Voiron (Isère) he made bars called *"grands Crus, à base de fèves d'origine pure et garantie."* It was the beginning of a revolution that continues to bear fruit.

MILK: PAY ATTENTION TO THE PERCENTAGES

If for dark chocolate attention is focused mainly on the origin, for milk chocolate the interesting thing is the percentage of cocoa it contains. By law, such percentage can be quite low, around 25%, with the result of a sweet and free of aromaticity taste. Fortunately, now the artisan industries and chocolatiers produce bars with much higher percentages, as in the case of Venchi, which won the gold tablet in the category, with 47% Milk chocolate obtained from the selection of particular Venezuelan beans with strong hints of cocoa and cream, together with milk from pastures of the Maritime Alps.

There are also new processing technologies, with the use of fresh milk with high temperature vaporization, instead of powdered milk: the first to use this method was a German firm, Jordan & Timeo, in 1839, with a "donkey milk chocolate," but it was not successful because it was difficult to preserve. The first commercial type of milk bar dates back to 1875 and is attributed to the Swiss Daniel Peter, who became a chocolatier in his father-in-law's company François-Louis Cailler: At the beginning he had difficulty removing the water from the milk, which deteriorated the product, then with the help of Henry Nestlé, maker of powdered milk, he succeeded in his intent.

GIANDUIA: FROM TURIN TO THE REST OF THE WORLD

This type of chocolate was added much later to the *Codex Alimentarius* because the African countries members of the FAO committee opposed it, as the cocoa allowed was less than 35%, the minimum chocolate threshold, and they considered it a sort of surrogate. Finally, an official of the Association of Confectionery industrialists convinced them, by bringing a box of Gianduiotti to a meeting in Switzerland in 2001. They were won over. The first wrapped chocolates in the world were born in 1867, with the addition of hazelnuts to the cocoa mass: their quantity must be between 20 and 40%. There are also bars: check if the percentage of hazelnuts is shown on the label, the higher the percentage the higher the quality, even in spreads.

WHITE IS NOT REALLY CHOCOLATE

While some like white chocolate, it is actually used today especially in the confectionary business, because it is very ductile and blends well with other ingredients. Purists rightly recall that technically it isn't chocolate, even if it is admitted by the *Codex*, as it has no cocoa mass among the ingredients, but only cocoa butter, sugar and powdered milk. In the history of the Food of the Gods, white chocolate is quite recent: it was created in Switzerland in the 1930s by Nestlé, who marketed it in 1936 with the famous Galak bar. Its taste also depends very much on the quality of the added vanilla.

RUBY: THE PINK SIDE OF CHOCOLATE

The target is very precise: Millennial generation passionate users of Instagram. In just a few months, there were hundreds of photos posted with sweets and bars with the hashtag *#rubychocolate*. Presented on September 5, 2017 in Shanghai, China, the Ruby RB1 is a new type of chocolate developed in thirteen years of experimentation by the Belgian-Swiss group Barry Callebaut, the result of a patented processing of particular cocoa beans "cultivated in Ivory Coast, Ecuador and Brazil."

Presented by the company as "the fourth type of chocolate," it is actually very similar to white chocolate, but has hints of berries with a final acidity. The percentage of cocoa – in *couverture* drops – is 47%, with 28% of powdered milk. The company ensures that no other ingredients or dyes are added.

Experts believe that optical reading machines choose certain lighter or more violet cocoa beans and their short fermentation (less than three days) is blocked with citric acid.

MODICANO: THE FIRST EUROPEAN PGI

There is a kind of Food of the Gods, actually it is a way of processing it, which in October 2018 obtained the PGI European certification: it is the "chocolate of Modica," which is obtained by mixing the Cocoa mass (minimum 50%) with the sugar in a "cold" process (below 120 °F or 50 °C, prescribed by the specifications), without the conching phase. Additionally, spices can be added such as cinnamon, vanilla, chilli, nutmeg. Natural aromas such as citrus, fennel, jasmine and ginger are also allowed. The characteristic of this product is the graininess on the palate, since sugar does not melt at that temperature.

The purpose of PGI protection, the first in Europe for a chocolate (in Turin a group of Chocolatiers are trying to obtain it for the Gianduiotto), is to protect the local artisans and promote the territory. According to some, it was above all a skillful action of territorial marketing, even if the "pioneers" of this activity in Modica, in particular the Ruta family of the Dolceria Bonajuto, are actually against this disciplinary, considered too vast and trivial, especially for the rules on the origins of cocoa. In recent years, in fact, thanks to media coverage, in Modica a myriad of laboratories has popped up that simply mix ingredients of industrial origin. And so, a provocative label made by the purists has already been created, stating: "chocolate from a town near Ragusa."

DESSERT-CHOCOLATE BARS

On the shelves of supermarkets all over the world, new variations of the bars are proliferating: filled – with tiramisu, crème brûlé, fig, ginger, yogurt, marzipan, coconut, etc. – or with special ingredients: dried or candied fruit, coffee, tea.

It is a trend that has given a new definition to this category of chocolate, not yet registered in the *Codex*, as "dessert style." Maybe they have little to do with real chocolate, but they are certainly tempting if you want to try new tasty experiences.

113 top - Piedmont GPI hazelnuts of different sizes: chocolatiers look for the largest ones because they have a better degree of maturation.

THE NOCCIOLATO

One of the most irresistible specialties of modern Chocolaterie can be obtained from the combination of whole toasted hazelnuts and *Theobroma cacao*: the nocciolato. This is a characteristic dark chocolate – or white or milk chocolate – bar, from whose surface emerge round and inviting *Avellane* nuts: their tasting is a sensory experience that allows you to identify two flavors which are perfectly complementary.

The processing of these bars is very different from that of gianduia chocolate, in which the hazelnuts, reduced to very fine grains, are mixed and conched together with the cocoa mass. The quality of the raw material is fundamental to get a good nocciolato. The hazelnuts must have a regular shape, an intense fragrance and a sweet but decisive taste: the roasting must be balanced so that their characteristic notes are not lost. The chocolate must not have a too low percentage of cocoa, otherwise its aroma would be overpowered.

This type of chocolate is very energetic, as hazelnuts are a sort of superfood with many positive nutritional elements: they reduce the risk of cardiovascular diseases, according to some studies lower bad cholesterol and are rich in vitamin E, which protects the skin from the negative effects of ultraviolet rays.

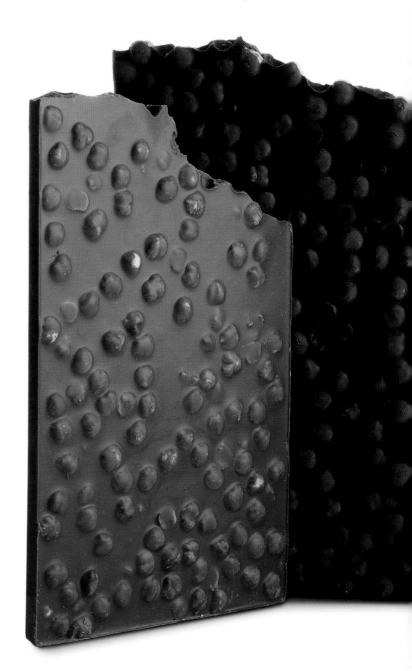

EASTER EGGS, BELLS, TEDDY BEARS, BUNNIES

It seems that the idea of the surprise inside a platinum and diamond egg came to Tsar Alexander III of Russia in 1883, who commissioned it to the master goldsmith Peter Carlo Fabergé for his wife Marija Fedorovna, princess of Denmark. Today, chocolate Easter eggs are one of the great businesses of chocolate artisans, while Ferrero has concentrated on children's eggs sold all year round, with a small toy inside: the invention of the Kinder surprise egg, created by manager William Salice, dates back to 1974. While bunnies and teddy bears are preferred in the UK and Germany, Lindt's Gold Bunny, born in 1952, is a worldwide Swiss icon. The Easter tradition of the *cloches en chocolat* continues in France and Belgium. It is not easy to determine

when chocolate Easter eggs were born: France, the United Kingdom and Italy all compete for paternity. The French chocolate historians Katherine Khodorowsky and Hervé Robert tell of how a French tinsmith craftsman began to sell chocolate molds in Paris in 1832 and in a short time the shop windows were filled with eggs and bells at Easter. The English company Cadbury (now Gruppo Mondelēz) claims to have produced them on an industrial scale since 1875, while in Italy a certain widow Giambone from Turin, is mentioned, who apparently made two shells in chocolate, then joined together to form an egg. Today chocolate eggs are more and more decorated with handmade motifs by skilled masters – in Italy one of the leaders was the Sicilian Guido Bellissima, active in Turin until the 1980s – or with daring interpretations of modern design.

CONSUMPTION FIGURES

According to data from Coabisco, the European organization of confectionery industries, the Swiss and German are the most enthusiastic consumers of chocolate: around 22 lbs (10 kg) per capita a year. Also, sales are growing steadily even in Asia, Oceania and Eastern Europe, in those countries that are discovering a passion for these products which are far from their food traditions.

In the most industrialized nations, like the United States, UK, France, and Italy, consumers are now making more healthy choices, now preferring dark chocolate and mono-origin chocolate instead of milk chocolate bars. However, Switzerland, Belgium, and Germany – according to Euromonitor estimates – are not losing any ground and remain firmly faithful to all forms of *Theobroma cacao*.

THE CHOCOLATE BOX CATALOGUE

We must be thankful to the Swiss chocolatier Jean Neuhaus, emigrated to Brussels, if today we can open a box of chocolates with delight, and experience this pleasure for the eyes and then for the taste-buds: it all happened in 1912, and three years later his wife created the *ballotin*, the cardboard box to contain those works of art made with the Food of the Gods.

But why are they called pralines? It is a French story that takes us to a small town, a two hour's drive south of Paris: Montargis. Here, in 1636, the cook of the Duke of Choiseul, count of Plessis-Praslin, had a small accident in the kitchen: the almonds that he had peeled to prepare a dessert ended up in the pan of freshly caramelized sugar. The Duke tasted them, and was instantly conquered, and in his honor, they became famous as *prasline*. A few years later, the chef opened his own pastisserie shop, Maison Mazet, which is still in business today and produces the *véritable prasline*. Since then not only the small crunchy bites made from almonds, but the whole production of *bon bon* has been known as "pralines."

Chocolates are mainly of two types: those with hollow body, filled with caramel, cream, crispy, marzipan or with *torroncino* or, however, with a mixture of chocolate, cocoa butter, hazelnuts or almonds, without the cream; and those based on a *ganache* made with chocolate mixed with cream, and/or butter, and perfumed with spices, essences, coffee, tea etc.

The variety of these small surprises of pleasure has no equal. They are mainly Belgian, French and Italian, with some Swiss intrusions. Some of these have a precise birth date and are linked to a brand, others are common heritage of European patisserie. They can be distinguished according to their filling. *Boiling or caramel* is defined as the filling made from sugar and cream or butter: typical of the Belgian patisserie. The *crunchy* is a modern version of the specialty born in Montargis, France, in the mid-17th century: almonds or hazelnuts or pistachios blended with caramelized sugar and covered with chocolate.

With the term *fondant* we identify a sweet, soft filling, like the one flavored with mint and enclosed between two sheets of dark chocolate that makes the English go crazy. When using *liqueur*, the hollow body containing it will be lined with a sugar coating so that it does not spill. The heart of a *bon bon* on the other hand is filled with marzipan made with almond paste and sugar: the Austrian boule dedicated to Mozart is one example. The *torroncino* is not really a praline but, as it is covered with chocolate, it invariably brings back to memory joyful childhood moments and never confessed sins of gluttony.

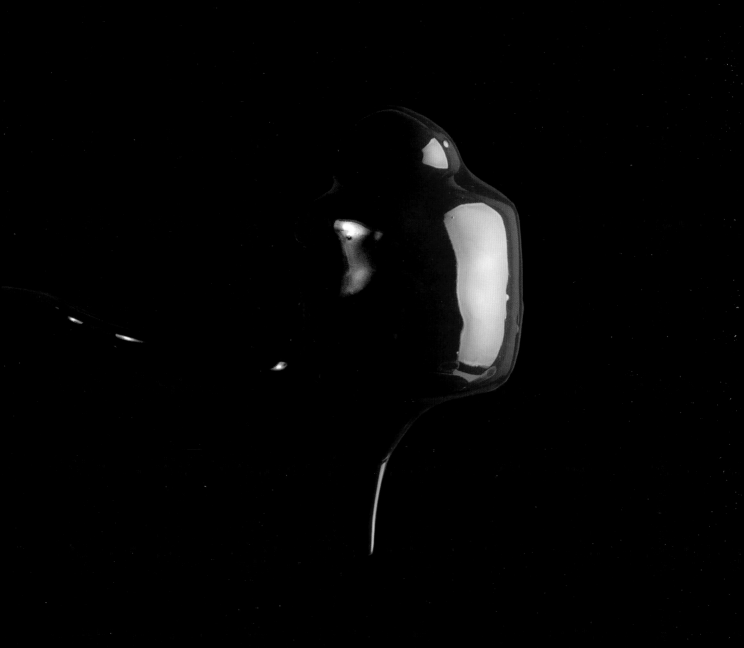

Over time, some types of chocolates have been registered, and are now found on trays in the windows of almost every chocolaterie. Here is a list of the main ones:

AFTER EIGHT

After eight o'clock in the evening you can definitely indulge yourself. This typically British chocolate is a thin mint fondant covered in dark chocolate.

ALKEKENGI

Technically it is not a chocolate, but a coated fruit: it is an orange colored berry, its scientific name is *Physalis alkekengi*, which in winter, in the patisseries of Milan and recently throughout northern Italy, is covered with dark chocolate. A pleasant contrast with the acidity of the fruit.

BACIO

It is perhaps the most famous Italian chocolate, also for the little notes with love phrases inside the wrapping. It was created in 1922 by Perugina: it has a gianduia filling with a whole hazelnut at the top and at first, it was called *cazzotto* ("punch") for its shape. Its name changed with the advertisement designed by Seneca, which took its cue from the Hayez painting *The Kiss* (i.e. *Il bacio* in Italian).

BOERO AND PREFERITO

This is a great classic: a liquor cherry (Cognac, Maraschino) covered with chocolate. In Italy, the version with the petiole is called *boero*, and the one without it, *preferito*. Its origins are Hungarian, and can be traced back to the end of the 19th century, in the patisserie founded in 1884 by the Swiss Emil Gerbeaud.

120 - A delicious praline just immersed in a chocolate bath by the master chocolatier.

CHOCOLATE SOMMELIER

121

CREMINO

It's all a matter of layers: there are three in the original version created in Turin by Ferdinando Baratti, who, together with his partner Edoardo Milano, opened a confectionery shop with laboratory in 1858. Gianduia is alternated with milk or coffee or lemon chocolate: the artisans make them with a special square called "a guitar," which allows to cut the mixture into regular squares.

CRI CRI

They look like candies, because they're wrapped the same way. They were launched in Turin during the *Belle Époque*: they are chocolate balls with a whole toasted hazelnut in the center, then covered with dark chocolate and colored sugar grains, called *mompariglia*.

RUM CUNEESE

It is a very greedy and widespread specialty, especially in Piedmont. It is said to have been created in Dronero, near Cuneo, and was registered in 1923 by the

Arione patisserie. Ernest Hemingway also fell in love with it. It is made with two semispherical discs of light meringue, joined by a special, rum-flavored chocolate spread, then covered with dark chocolate. Pietro Cussino in the 1950s adapted the recipe by pouring the cream into a pure chocolate shell and allowing his Cuban rum to be better preserved, and so to be distributed both in Italy and abroad.

DRAGÉE

It is a small chocolate with a heart of candied orange, an almond, a hazelnut, a berry covered with chocolate: its production started at the beginning of the 20th century by the Venchi factory in Turin. The *dragée* managed to win the gold medal at the Italian General Exhibition in 1884.

FRUIT DE MAR

The shell-shaped chocolate, with a filling of praline and marbled coating, is the flagship of the Guylian brand, and is one of the iconic specialties of Belgian pralines. It was born from the romance between the chocolatier Guy Foubert and his wife Liliane, who he married in 1958: a fusion of their names, the brand is now present in 140 countries.

GIANDUIOTTO

It's the gianduia chocolate born in Turin in the middle of the 19th century, dedicated to the carnival character of Turin. It has an inverted boat shape and can be realized with three different processes: by hand with two knives, cast in molds or extruded by a machine. Its original ingredients are: hazelnuts, cocoa and sugar. The original recipe added variants with powdered milk or aromatized with coffee, chilli or other spices.

LINDOR

It is the most renowned Lindt *bon bon*, born in Zurich in 1967: technically it is a sphere formed by two hollow bodies with a soft filling. After the original milk version, about twenty different variants have been created with different fillings: strawberry, cappuccino, caramel, mango, citrus, etc.

MOZARTKULGEN

They were created in honor of Wolfgang Amadeus Mozart in 1890 from Salzburg confectioner Paul Fürst: he did not register the name of his invention, and now many produce the "Mozart balls." It is a boule of chocolate filled with pistachio marzipan, and is still handmade in the laboratory where it was born.

MENDIANT

It is a chocolate waffle on which four different types of dried fruit are placed, the color recalls that of the robes worn by the friars of four mendicant orders: almonds for the Dominicans; hazelnuts for the Franciscans; figs for the Carmelites; berries for the Hermits of St. Augustine.

NAPOLITAIN

It is a square mini-bar for tasting or served with a cup of espresso coffee, weighing 5 grams, individually wrapped.

NOUGATINE

Created in 1922 in Turin by the Idea company, founded by financier Riccardo Gualino, they were brought to success by Venchi-Unica (which incorporated the Idea) and then by Venchi: they are crunchy oval shaped *bon bon* with Piedmont hazelnuts chopped and caramelized, covered in dark chocolate.

PALET D'OR

A round disc of dark chocolate covered with a gold leaf and filled with a coffee *ganache*. It was created in France at the end of the 19th century by Bernard Serardy, confectioner of Moulins, ancient capital of the Bourbonnais. Unfortunately, the craftsman was unable to defend the registration of his specialty and the *Palet d'or* is now the heritage of all the chocolaterie in the world.

ROCHER

It is a classic of Belgian and French patisserie: a heart consisting of a whole hazelnut, covered with a crispy wafer or a "praliné" of almonds, finished with a layer of chocolate and hazelnut grain.

TRUFFLE

It is a small, soft ball made with a chocolate ganache, sprinkled with cocoa powder: it takes its name from the shape, reminiscent of the famous underground mushroom.

ZEST

This is basically a slice of candied orange peel. It has been the typical production of a small town near Turin, Carignano, since the 17th century. It is a greedy delight when it is covered with dark chocolate, a procedure also done with other candied fruits: lemon, pumpkin, ginger, etc.

126 - The truffle has a soft heart wrapped in bitter cocoa powder.

THE ART OF PATISSERIE

The confectionary world began to express itself with chocolate between the end of the 18th century and the early 19th century, achieving astonishing results especially in Austria, France and Germany. Seductive cakes and irresistible pastries triumphed in the sparkling windows of these famous sanctuaries of gluttony. The specialties made with *Theobroma cacao* are countless and it is impossible to make a complete catalogue. We will merely point out those with a "brand" of origin and a fairly certain date of birth; many of them are linked to romantic love stories, to the gluttony of princesses and queens, and even to long legal disputes.

ASSABESE (CIRCA 1915)

It is a historic cake, made by two discs of chocolate pastry alternating with as many discs of chocolate sponge cake, both lightly soaked in rum, filled with a hazelnut cream and hazel and dark chocolate ganache. Its name is a legacy of Italian colonial victories: Assayab Bay, in Eritrea, "conquered" in 1882. Two years later a group of Dancali, an Eritrean tribe, was brought as a "trophy" to the international exhibition of Turin. Their presence aroused much curiosity and inspired many confectionery products in Italy: biscuits, licorice treats, etc. Probably the first to prepare the cake was the pastry chef Gustavo Pfatisch, of Alsace origin, when he opened his elegant shop in Turin, in 1915. The patisserie, which still produces it, is one of the Historical Places of Italy.

BAROZZI (1907)

Low, compact, rectangular in shape, it is handmade according to a secret recipe with dark chocolate, butter, peanuts, almonds and coffee. It was created in 1907 in Vignola, a town between Modena and Bologna famous for its cherries, by the pastry chef Eugenio Gollini, who dedicated it to the illustrious fellow citizen Jacopo Barozzi, architect of the 16th century.

BROWNIE (1898)

This soft cake made from flour, butter, chocolate and eggs, cut into squares and covered with a glossy apricot or dark glaze, is one of the most popular cakes in the United States: it can be accompanied with a little cream, a scoop of ice cream or a coffee. There are many versions of brownies (so-called for their brown color) also according to the city they come from. The origins are placed in Chicago, in the hotel Palmer House, in 1898: still today the hotel prepares the original recipe with an apricot glaze. The first recipe was published a few years later in Boston, in 1904, but involves the addition of chopped walnuts.

BÛCHE DE NOËL (CIRCA 1945)

In French homes during the new-year festivities the "Christmas Log," is a must which according to tradition was prepared in 1945 by a Parisian pastry chef to celebrate the first Christmas without war. It is now widespread in some French speaking countries, such as Quebec, Belgium and Lebanon. It consists of a thin rectangular sponge cake, filled with chocolate cream, which is rolled up and covered with dark icing; but there are different versions.

CAPRESE (CIRCA 1920)

It's a cake that dates back to the 1920s by a pastry chef from the island of Capri. The ingredients are: chopped dark chocolate, chopped peeled almonds, sugar, butter and eggs. It doesn't contain flour, because, it is said, that the chef forgot to add it.

DECADENCE CAKE (CIRCA 1980)

Popular in the United States in the early 1980s, this flour-free cake is considered the "decadent dream" of all chocoholics: it is prepared by mixing dark chocolate and butter in equal quantities, with added cocoa powder, eggs and cream. It can be served with a raspberry sauce.

DEVIL'S FOOD CAKE (1901)

The recipe for this chocolate cake, which every American housewife simply knows as "the devil's food" (in reference to the "sinful" origins of cocoa), was first published in 1901 in Milwaukee, Wisconsin in one of the longest-living cookbooks in the states, The *"Settlement" Cook Book*. It is composed of three very dark layers of chocolate sponge cake, alternated with soft whipped cream. The cookbook, which was intended for immigrants in the United States, was adopted as the basic text of American Jewish cuisine, with many editions up to the present day.

130 - Brownies, very popular in the United States, are said to have been born in Chicago.

DOBOSTORTE (1885)

This Hungarian cake was made for the Budapest Exposition of 1885 and bears the name of its inventor, the pastry chef Carl József Dobos. It is a very greedy specialty, consisting of six layers of sponge cake, interspersed with a filling of butter cream and chocolate, with a shiny caramel coating.

FORESTA (CIRCA 1920)

It is a log made of thin chocolate sheets, joined like many trunks. It was created in the 1920s by the Neapolitan patisserie Gay Odin, founded in 1894 by Isidoro Odin, a Piedmontese chocolatier, with his wife Onorina Gay. Several shops are still in business with the Gay-Odin sign in Naples, Milan and Rome.

The name of this cake is inspired by the "mud" of the Mississippi River, in the south of the United States. it is considered a classic of the American "southern" cuisine. It is a leavened chocolate cake, which has the characteristic of being soft in the middle: it has a rather dense cocoa sauce base, reminiscent of mud, often accompanied by scoops of vanilla ice cream.

132-133 - The Mississippi Mud Pie achieved its greatest success in the 1970s.

SACHER-TORTE (1832)

Without a doubt, it is the most famous chocolate cake in the world, emblem of Austria's contribution to the Food of the Gods. Its history is marked by legal disputes and today by rather casual interpretations in all the patisseries of the five continents. It was created, according to tradition, by Franz Sacher (who was just sixteen years old) in 1832 when he was at the service of Chancellor von Metternich. The claim of its creation however came fifty years later and according to some historians some French chefs also contributed to its origins. In 1848 Sacher opened his patisserie shop in Vienna, and then in 1876 his son Eduard inaugurated the hotel near the Opera that is still in operation today.

In the 1930s, a legal dispute broke out with another patisserie shop in Vienna, Demel, who started the production of a cake very similar to the Sacher. The Sachers won: only their patisserie can use the original brand *Original Sacher-Torte*. So, in the Viennese capital you can find two versions: in that of Demel the apricot jam is on the surface of the cake, under the final glaze, instead of in the middle as in the Sacher-Torte.

SAVOY CAKE (1713?)

Despite its name it is not a cake from Piedmont, but it has ancient Sicilian origins: in Palermo the most renowned patisserie shops continue to make it. The local legend wants the dessert to be prepared on December 24, 1713 in Palermo, when Vittorio Amedeo II of Savoy, thanks to the Treaty of Utrecht, was crowned King of Sicily: a title that he retained for a few years, until the island returned to the Habsburgs. Some sources cite instead the nuns of a convent of Catania as the creators. Today the recipe includes three discs of sponge cake, interspersed with a filling of gianduia cream, all covered with a dark glaze with the inscription "Savoy."

137 - The Austrian Sacher-Torte is perhaps the most widespread chocolate dessert, prepared by pastry chefs all over the world.

SCHWARZWÄLD (1915)

In the gourmand geography of the Food of the Gods Germany occupies a prominent place thanks to this dessert, which in German is also called *Schwarzwälder Kirschtorte*, that is "cherry cake of the Black Forest." It is supposed to have been invented by pastry chef Josef Keller from Bad Godesberg, a district in Bonn, in 1915. It is very rich: it has more layers of chocolate sponge cake, interspersed with whipped cream, it is completely covered with whipped cream enriched with flakes of dark chocolate decorated with candied cherries.

SETTEVELI (1997)

It is the pride of Italian patisserie because it won the *Coupe du Monde de la pâtisserie* in 1997 in Lyon. The Italian team that won the coveted trophy was composed of: Christian Beduschi (of Cortina d'ampezzo), Luigi Biasetto (of Padua) and Luca Mannori (of Prato). The coach of the team was Iginio Massari, the founder of the *Accademia Maestri Pasticceri Italiani* ("Master Italian Confectioners Academia"). It is a modern multi-layered cake, very imitated, but registered and "original" only in the four patisseries of the winners who competed in the international competition. Coated with a glossy glaze and decorated with gold leaves, the interior houses a soft chocolate mousse interspersed with a praline hazelnut bavarese, with chocolate puff pastry and a crispy cereal base.

TARTUFATA (1907)

A "soft drapery" of light chocolate leaves characterizes this very popular cake. This is how it is defined in Vercelli in the *pasticceria* Follis, opened in 1907, which keeps its tradition going. It is made with three discs of sponge cake moistened with rum and maraschino, filled with hazelnut whipped cream and a coating of hazelnut grains around the edges. It is claimed by Vercelli, but the year of its birth is uncertain. In Turin, from the middle of the 20th century the patisserie Pfatisch, enticed its customers with a sweet Sunday cake called festive, very similar to the truffle, but with more chocolate at the base.

TENERINA (BEGINNING OF THE 20TH CENTURY)

Originally from Ferrara, probably at the beginning of the 20th century it was called Montenegrin cake or queen of Montenegro cake, in honor of Elena of Montenegro, wife of King Victor Emmanuel III of Savoy. It is composed of dark chocolate, sugar, eggs and flour: it has a crispy surface and a soft heart.

TIRAMISU (1950s)

It is certainly the most famous Italian dessert in the world, although it is quite recent. The word tiramisu is indeed present, as a gastronomic Italianism, in 23 languages of the world. It was created in Tolmezzo in the restaurant of the hotel Roma by the hands of Norma Pielli (between 1954 and 1959, as testified by the first written evidence), then it was registered in Treviso in the restaurant Alle Becchiere (1970) by the pastry chef Loli Linguanotto. The first recipe published in a cookbook dates back to 1983. It is a soft dessert, made with ladyfingers soaked in coffee, mascarpone cream with beaten egg and an inevitable sprinkled finish of abundant cocoa.

ZURIGO (CIRCA 1930)

It is similar in appearance to the Black Forest, but differs in its execution and is now registered by a patisserie shop in Pinerolo (Turin) that defends its originality. It was conceived by the pastry chef Giuseppe Castìno, in the 1930s in the Piedmontese town that housed the famous Cavalry School of the royal army. This was frequently visited by the Princess Iolanda of Savoy, the daughter of King Victor Emmanuel III, who one day commissioned a special cake to be brought to Zurich for a visit to some Swiss friends. After the compliments received, Castìno put it in production, calling it Zurigo cake. It is composed of a waffle of cocoa shortbread, with filling of Chantilly cream enriched with flakes of nougat and dark chocolate. On the surface the white glaze is decorated with chocolate leaves and cherries under spirit.

RECOGNIZED
BENEFICIAL EFFECTS

During the 18th century and until the middle of the 19th century, chocolate was considered a cure-all for health and even a medicine. It is testified by Brillat Savarin, author of the fundamental treatise in the history of gastronomy, *The Physiology of Taste*, published posthumously in 1826: "if any man has drunk a little too deeply from the cup of physical pleasure; if he has spent too much time at his desk that should have been spent asleep; if his fine spirits have temporarily become dulled; if he finds the air too damp, the minutes too slow, and the atmosphere too heavy to withstand; if he is obsessed by a fixed idea which bars him from any freedom of thought: if he is any of these poor creatures, we say, let him be given a good pint of amber-flavored chocolate."

Old wives' tales or truth? Don't worry, and do continue to cultivate your passion for *Theobroma cacao* without feelings of guilt and anxieties of about diabetes: it has been proven that chocolate does not contain cholesterol (which is present only in foods of animal origin), it is not a drug that is addictive, neither does it cause tooth decay or obesity.

Recent scientific discoveries have brought to light many positive properties: dark chocolate with a high percentage of cocoa is an antioxidant thanks to flavonoids, it liquifies the blood and therefore makes a good contribution to keeping the arteries clean. It is also an effective stress reliever, thanks to serotonin and phenylethylamine, but also a good stimulant due to the effect of theobromine.

HEART AND BRAIN

Cocoa has a high content of flavonoids, natural chemical compounds known for their healthy properties. They are present in many plants and can be assimilated by drinking a cup of green tea or a glass of red wine. A mug of hot chocolate, however, has double the flavonoid content of a Barolo or a Bordeaux and triple of a steaming cup of Assam tea. Some American research has shown that the daily intake of a certain amount of dark chocolate can reduce the main risk factors of cardiovascular disease.

Further studies carried out in Italy have highlighted the beneficial neuroprotective effects of the Food of the Gods on the brain, because it can increase attention levels, the ability to understand and even memory.

We can therefore argue, and even emphasize a little, that taking controlled doses of chocolate is good for the heart and brain: you should not consider it a medicine as was believed two centuries ago, or replace it with drugs. But it is certainly an aid to be reckoned with. Analyzing the mineral components of cocoa, we find the presence of beneficial substances for our organism, such as magnesium, phosphorus, potassium and some vitamins.

STRESS RELIEVER AND STIMULANT

We owe to an Italian-American scientist, Daniele Piomelli, the discovery that dark chocolate (and only this) contains anandamide, also known as the molecule of joy. It is a lipid mediator and a cannabinoid present in our brain, which stimulates it. The term anandamide derives from Sanskrit *ānanda*, a word meaning "bliss." According to an American neuroscientist, chocolate is an excellent antidepressant, because it activates the brain receptors in the reward system. And similarly, we can also mention serotonin: it is a neurotransmitter contained in cocoa that regulates mood, sleep, appetite and even the sexual sphere.

The last beneficial effect is the stimulant one, as is well known by sportsmen. Indeed, in chocolate there are two substances: caffeine, in a dose however ten times less than in a cup of coffee, therefore without side-affects to sleep; and theobromine, which is only contained in cocoa, from which it takes its name. It seems that theobromine blocks the hormone of fear, that is adrenaline, which happens when we are in stressful situations. So, apart from relaxing us it also stimulates us into action.

FIVE SENSES
FOR
TASTING

There are certain parameters that a sommelier uses when tasting chocolate. Experience, professionalism and sensory analysis are also needed. It is almost an exact science, even if the subjective element always prevails. The tasting of a wine consists in several phases – visual, olfactory and taste – and this is also true for chocolate. We change the techniques, the methods of evaluation, the senses involved. Certainly, experience is a determining factor: as with all foods, our senses are based on memories. If the scent of a dark bar is reminiscent of ripe fruit or tobacco or coffee, the taste accordingly goes to seek the scents of sweetness, bitterness, acidity comparing them with those stored in our brain.

In order to understand the Food of the Gods properly it's not enough just to love it, you also have to know how to taste it. The first rule to keep in mind when tasting a chocolate is to involve all the five senses. The second rule is concentration: one thing is to eat chocolates in front of the television, another is the sensory analysis of a bar of dark mono-origin chocolate. Third rule: the Food of the Gods should not be chewed, but instead let to dissolve slowly in the mouth, in the center of the tongue against the palate.

To better perceive the about five hundred aromas that *Theobroma cacao* contains in its fava beans, it is advisable for your experience to take place away from meals: there are those who do it as soon as they wake up, after drinking a glass of water, at six o'clock in the morning so as not to be disturbed, but perhaps this is a bit excessive... It is better if there are no predominant smells in the room and the temperature shouldn't be too high, around 68-71 °F (20-22 °C). Also, if you smoke, forget the cigarettes for at least an hour before tasting and refrain from wearing any perfume.

The tasting of a chocolate bar can be done with various comparisons:

- Mono-origin chocolate with cocoa from only one country, but produced by different companies;
- Chocolates of the same type (milk, dark, etc.) with different percentages of cocoa;
- Chocolates of different types (white, milk, gianduia, dark) of the same producer;
- Chocolate or pralines of the same producer with different fillings.

Some believe that, for a more objective judgement, it is necessary to follow an "uphill" tasting path: from the less prized and sweeter (with a lower percentage of cocoa) to the more complex and bitter. But it might be interesting to start with the shock of a crushed toasted cocoa bean, to prepare the palate and then to pass on to the various bars.

SIGHT

Get your mouth watering! Focus on the color and the texture of the chocolate: check if it is shiny or if it has a matte patina. The color must be light ocher for milk or gianduia specialties and mahogany for the dark, with different shades of brown, but not black. If the bar has reddish shades, it means that it has been made with good aromatic cocoa: Criollo is the lightest in color. To evaluate faults (stains, porosity, streaks) also observe the lower part, which must be shiny, an indication of good tempering. It is important that there are no white or grey outcrops of cocoa butter, an indication of incorrect preservation. Breaking a bar, it must break without crumbling and without presenting bubbles inside, indication of an imperfect crystallization.

HEARING

Don't be surprised, even hearing can be useful to understand if a chocolate is of good quality: break it near your ear to hear a pleasant "snap." The sound must be clear and distinct, not soft or dull.

TOUCH

It can be done in two ways: touch the surface of the bar with the fingertips of one hand, to perceive its silkiness or graininess due to the presence of *grué*, or the grain of cocoa in pieces; or in the mouth, with the tongue, to assess the melting rate of the chocolate, which must melt quickly to immediately give you all its aromaticity.

SMELL

There are experts who can recognize the type of *Theobroma cacao* just using their noses. You can reach this level by having gained a lot of experience. But there is an easy exercise to help you train: sniff, with your eyes closed, an industrial bar of dark with 50% cocoa, and then an artisan mono-origin at 75%. The first one gives a sweeter, vanilla scent, while the second will envelope you in a more profound complex aroma of cocoa. In milk chocolate the scent of caramel is generally prevalent, besides that of fresh cream, if it is of good quality. You can identify flaws with your nose too: if you smell a hint of cheese (not rare in certain raw or extreme products), it is the indication of a poorly-conched cocoa; worse, the smell of mold or rancid indicate the product has gone off. Using your sense of smell, you will be able to find some sensory memories: coffee, fresh fruit or dried fruit, wood, liquorice, honey, tobacco, spices.

TASTE

At last you have reached the most awaited and pleasant moment. You will find that it is a more complete and satisfactory experience if you involved the other senses first. However, the characteristics of a chocolate can only be analyzed by tasting it: intensity, richness, finesse, persistence, equilibrium. It is essential that the bar has a fair balance between sweet, bitter and sour. Finally, let yourself be surprised by the "aftertaste" that can arrive even after a few minutes of having let the chocolate melt in your mouth. It is what is called the "depth" or "length" of *Theobroma cacao*. You can also understand the texture: velvety (excellent), grainy (defect), pasty (but not too much) or dry (not pleasant). And do not be discouraged if at the first attempts, after reading these tips, you don't find all the nuances indicated: tasting makes perfect!

PERFECT HARMONY

In order for your taste buds to be enraptured by the symphony of aromatic chords present in a chocolate bar and to perceive above all the depth of the cocoa *cru*, it is a good rule to drink a glass of water first. If you prefer to indulge in the game of pleasure, you will be amazed and conquered by the surprising gastronomic affinity cocoa has with some drinks and many spices. White chocolate, for example, is enhanced by aromas such as vanilla, pink pepper, cardamom or even paired with strawberries. Milk or gianduia chocolate go perfectly well with all dried fruit. Dark chocolate finds its harmony with chilli, nutmeg, acidic red fruits.

It was once argued that with the Food of the Gods you should not drink wine, but now many professional tasters have shown that it is not so. If you want to accompany a chocolate dessert with a wine, you must break every taboo: experiments are welcome and open to many possible sensory experiences.

COFFEE

Coffee beans grow from small shrubs originating in Ethiopia (arabica) and Central Africa. Just like cocoa, they must be roasted to develop their aromatic qualities, which they transfer into a hot beverage. For its stimulating properties, coffee is often compared to hot chocolate.

Many say that coffee and chocolate do not go well together, because the strong aroma of coffee, characterized by a certain acidity, ends up prevailing over the "longer" hidden shades of chocolate. This is not always true. In fact, the Italian tradition of the late 18th century left us two very invigorating drinks, that prove a successful marriage between the two, served in glass: the *bicerin* from Turin and the *barbajada* from Milan, directly descended from the *bavaroise*.

In Turin, a small chocolaterie is still active in the square of the town center, which is the constant destination of tourists, it is "Caffè Al Bicerin" opened in 1763. It is an elegant room with original furnishings in which the *bicerin*, which gave its name to the room, is served, distinguished by three layers: coffee, hot chocolate and milk cream. The drink, which takes its name from the small glasses without a handle in which it was served (precisely *bicerin*), is drunk without stirring.

Milan instead claims the birthright of *barbajada* or *barbagliata*: it is a recipe similar to *bicerin*, with an addition of tasty whipped cream. The name of the drink recalls the lyric impresario of La Scala theatre, Domenico Barbaja (1778-1841) who liked to enjoy it and seems to have contributed to its creation. The origin could derive from the *bavaroise*, a drink

made from tea, milk and alcohol, prepared, over the years, with some variants, such as the addition of coffee and chocolate. It is not to be confused with the "Bavarese," a pudding made with English cream, whipped cream and jelly. The "Bavarese" is supposed to have been made in the early 18th century in France by cooks serving the Wittelsbach, ruling house in Bavaria.

A famous specialty of international chocolate are coffee *bon bon*, made in three ways. Firstly, with coffee in a liquid form, inside a shell of dark chocolate; secondly, in a creamy form, as one of the layers of a cremino or as an ingredient of a ganache inside a praline; and finally, as a *dragée*, the simple bean covered with dark or milk chocolate.

Coffee is a "difficult" ingredient for desserts. There are sweets in which its traditional acidity is mitigated by the cocoa: like the Opéra French cake, the Italian tiramisu, the Piedmontese *bônet*.

When you want to accompany a cup of coffee with a chocolate, know that an elegant Ethiopean mocha is indicated for dark chocolate; a Colombian coffee is ideal for cakes or white chocolate mousse; and the beans of Santo Domingo are good for the Pralinato.

All over the world it is increasingly common to enter a bar and find that the Italian espresso is served with a napolitain: that little bite of chocolate enhances the pleasure of coffee, and can even be used instead of sugar.

TEA

The most widespread beverage in the world, tea is prepared thanks to the leaves of plants originating in China and India that are dried, sometimes also fermented (black tea) and then infused. Two main qualities are produced – the Chinese and the Assam – although the connoisseur knows how to recognize a thousand types. The combination with the Food of the Gods is rather customary and "easy": either in the form of a drink to taste together with a chocolate, or as an ingredient for a delicate praline.

The variations and combinations are endless. A mono-origin equatorial napolitain of Arriba, for example, can be tasted together with an Earl Grey tea with notes of bergamot, a good combination. Instead, by contrast, the sweetness of a white chocolate can be accompanied by the bitter taste of a green matcha tea. For a praline, a Darjeeling with hints of almond is perfect, while a milk praline goes best with a Wulong, a fermented Chinese tea.

CHOCOLATE SOMMELIER

BEER

Until a few years ago, it seemed unusual, daring and even unseemly to combine hops with *Theobroma cacao*; but now, such combination is much loved by all its enthusiasts. It can be done in two ways: making artisan beer with cocoa, made with an infusion of fava beans during the "cooking," generally used for *stout* and *bock* beer; or by sipping a beer with a good alcoholic content while tasting chocolate.

Any advice? The *stout* beer, malt-based longer roasted and more alcoholic and bitter, generally has more "cocoa" and "coffee" aromas that are well matched with dark chocolate. But even here it is necessary to experiment with an open mind: the sweetness of a white chocolate praline, perhaps slightly spicy, can perfectly support by contrast a well structured and bitter porter or *barley wine beer*. Among the British beers, it is better to choose a high fermentation *real ale*.

Some artisans have made pralines in which milk chocolate is combined with a "bitter beer" filling. In Belgium, home to great trappist beers and excellent chocolates, there are many examples of *Belgian Beer Chocolates*, in the form of truffles, boule and filled shells.

WINE

For a long time, the suggestions for food and wine pairings used to put dark chocolate into the category of "unpairable" foods, thus neglecting the fact that some types of chocolate can actually make some very interesting tasting pairings. Gianduia chocolate, for instance, in which the organoleptic peculiarities of hazelnut and cocoa are blended, lends itself to exciting sensory combinations.

The covered gianduiotto, a specialty of Venchi, is a classic example: this dark chocolate at 56% with a filling of gianduia, can become the perfect partner of a Barolo or a Nebbiolo.

The dark chocolate alone could create an excessive contrast with the tannins present in the wine, causing excessive astringency and a bitter taste. The delicacy of the gianduia on the other hand harmonizes well with a wine of this body type, and the fats present in the hazelnut are perfectly balanced with the acidity of a Barolo.

A dark chocolate that confirms the exception to the rule is the fruity Venezuela, famous for its notes of ripe cherries, which goes well with Amarone, Sfursat or Montepulciano D'Abruzzo. Also a glass of sparkling wine, vinified according to the classic method (French Champagne, Italian Franciacorta or Trentodoc or Alta Langa), can make a tasty pairing with white chocolate with hazelnuts, almonds and salted pistachios or with a truffle with a sweet-salty finish. The Brut sparkling wine will seem to become satèn, transforming the tasting into a pleasant evolution of perfumes and flavors.

Natural sweet wines, like many intense and fruity Austrian *Prädikatswein*, some French *Muscat* of the Languedoc-Roussilon, and in Italy fresh and light wines like the Moscato d'Asti, the Asti Spumante, the Brachetto D'Acqui and the Malvasia of Castelnuovo Don Bosco: all these know how to enhance the gianduia bar or chocolate.

The combination of chocolate with all the *passito* wines is more consolidated, both with those from grapes left on the vines for over-maturation, and those left in bunches to wilt on the trellises of a cellar, like the Passito of Pantelleria, with a golden and warm color like the sun that heats the island, or the Aleatico

dell'Elba, fresh and fragrant with its scents of red fruits. The Passito of Pantelleria is better suited to accompany a sweet-salty chocolate such as a pistachio Chocaviar or a cremino, while the Aleatico goes better with a dark chocolate between 60 and 75%. Apart from the famous Italian *passito*, in Europe the most popular wines are the French Sauternes, the Hungarian Tokaj, the German and Austrian *Eiswein* (which in fact are not *passito*, but vinified by grapes harvested in winter and then "frozen"). These are among the sweetest and most dense wines in existence: they are excellent in contrast to a dark chocolate as well as to intense chocolates in blends such as Montezuma nibs or Chocaviar at 75%.

FORTIFIED WINES

Wines defined as "fortified" or "liquor" are those that receive an addition of alcohol during their maturation. Fortified wines are certainly advisable for both desserts and tastings, and are often used to make filled chocolates. In Europe, the best known are: in Portugal, port (based on arrested fermentation); in Spain, Jerez (Sherry in English); in France, Banyuls (in the south, near the Spanish border, excellent and very sought after) and the Pineau des Charentes (one third of Cognac liquor and two thirds of must, produced in the Dordogne); In Italy, Marsala and Barolo Chinato.

A rarity until a few decades ago, today the Barolo Chinato is experiencing a comeback, thanks to the Food of the Gods: it is an elixir born in the hills of the Langhe, in Piedmont, at the end of the 19th century. Thanks to the seasoning of spices added to the noble wine, characterized by scents and a red amber color, Barolo Chinato is a "lord" to sip in meditation with a dark napolitain. It is even more surprising when served cold as an aperitif and paired with citrus peel, candied and covered in chocolate.

The last frontier is the pairing with red vermouth of Turin, in the ancient formula (many small producers have sprung up): therefore, not only aperitif, but a surprising idea to accompany *Theobroma cacao*.

DISTILLED SPIRITS

Almost all distilled spirits go great with chocolate and were once the only suggested pairing, apart from the combination with Port.

Spirits refined in barrels form excellent associations with the Food of the Gods, thanks to the silky softness that they get from the long contact with wood. The world of spirits is even more extensive than that of fortified wines, but the combination with softer ones can give the most satisfaction to the palate. Thus, for example, between Armagnacs and French cognacs one must choose those with the acronym XO (Extra Old), aged more than six years. And, among the whiskies, it is preferable to choose – strictly in combination with dark chocolate – those of pure Scottish malt: peaty ones are perfect and they are to be tasted with bitter chocolate from a strong personality cocoa, such as a Forastero Nacional of Ecuador at 70% or an extra-dark cremino characterized by the notes of hazelnuts and almonds. Also great are American bourbons that, with their marked toasted smoky notes, go well with aromatic cocoa of great succulence like the filled aromatic cigar or the Montezuma nibs 75%.

Also, very popular are the great Japanese blended, which offer amazing combinations with dark chocolate: an "uphill" tasting of different percentages of cocoa, from 60% to 75%, is definitely suggested.

CHOCOLATE SOMMELIER

It is rum, distilled from cane sugar, that has always been the preferred union with chocolate: from central America we have *Ron* (the Spanish name) with twenty years of aging that offers delicious surprises with the right chocolate. How to choose? Based on experience, there are no general rules.

A correct tasting of dark chocolate in combination with a distillate requires the proper amount of time. Indeed, tasting means knowing and learning how to interpret the pairing: it must be a special moment, so it is necessary to create the right atmosphere. To taste the distillates correctly, it is necessary to also have fresh still water available. The ritual of the tasting is composed of three fundamental phases that involve smell, sight and taste.

Let's start with this path together:

- Pour about 1 fl oz (3cl) of distillate into a glass, preferably a goblet, to better appreciate the scents: bring it to your nose to seize the aromatic notes then rotate it to oxygenate it. Now, sniff it again and you will smell other aromas.

- Hold the glass up to the light, to admire its golden reflections, before tasting it hold the glass in your hands in a ritual that the tasters call "humanization"; the tasting is a ritual that will allow you to savor every drop slowly, so as to make the pleasure last for as long as possible.

- The first sip will explode in your mouth with all its power, you will taste the notes of black pepper, the salty flavor, but what will remain on your palate is the sensation of careful processing.

At this point, it is advisable to drink some still water to "clean" your mouth and prepare your palate for a new taste. This trick will allow you to seize new aromas from the distillate, such as dried fruit, flowers, smokiness, depending on the type of liquor. You are now ready to taste the chocolate, repeating the stages of involvement of the five senses illustrated on page 147.

You will first appreciate the scent of the chocolate, the cocoa powder, the sweetness of the sugar and vanilla, then you can chew it, before letting it melt in your mouth so as to develop the great combination of the expertly dosed different cocoa masses: you will be surprised by the balance of components that do not dry the palate without one sensation prevailing over the others. By increasing the percentage of cocoa, for example, with a blend of 75%, the result of the pairing will be different, because the structure of the chocolate is much more imposing, and even the color, dark mahogany, will give you with the same sensation. Taking a new chocolate bar and breaking it, bring it to your nose to smell the aromas that it releases: the smell will tend towards bitter chocolate, with a strong sensation of toasted cocoa, spicy with hints of nutmeg, ginger and background notes of vanilla and peanut butter. It will melt in your mouth much more slowly.

The aromatic complexity that the chocolate releases gradually will remind you much of what you smelt: the spices and notes of bitter cocoa. Each pairing will give you new sensations, leaving you the desire of trying again with different types of dark chocolate, different percentages of cocoa, for different aromatic experiences.

The Food of the Gods is characterized by aromatic notes that harmonize well with the herbs used by apothecaries. The pairing between spices and cocoa beans is as old as the history of chocolate: cinnamon, ginger, annatto, chilli, nutmeg are "natural friends" of *Theobroma cacao* and create perfect symphonic chords with it. The Modicano, linked to the Spanish tradition, is a striking example. In Tuscany many chocolatiers have been experimenting ever daring combinations in their pralines for years, especially with spicy chilli. In Arizona, in Phoenix, the Desert Botanical Park organizes a Chiles and Chocolate Festival, just like in Sydney, Australia, where the Nowra Chili & Chocolat Festival is held: in both events, chocolate is combined with the red berries in a thousand preparations to test the most hardened palates. In the United States, "chilli chocolate" sauce is used to accompany veal steak.

SPICES AND FRUIT

The use of fruit in chocolate is quite recent, but it is convincing more and more enthusiasts. Of course, nuts are perfect for cakes, creams, mousses and pastries: walnuts, hazelnuts, almonds, pistachios are used by skilled chocolatiers to create unforgettable *bon bon* or crispy bars. Since the 18th century, the precious crystal cake stands filled with candied citrus peel covered with chocolate have been an irresistible temptation to accompany a morning coffee or afternoon tea.

CHOCOLATE SOMMELIER

For fresh fruit, apart from the ritual of chocolate fondue, one can be guided by the mono-origin dark chocolates, in which the cocoa can undergo aromatic evolutions on the plantation very similar to the fruits we know. So, for instance a Sambirano cocoa from Madagascar has hints of plantain and banana, while the Porcelana of Venezuela has scents of ripe cherries, and the Piura cocoa of Peru emanates notes of lemon and citrus fruits.

The exotic passion fruit, the banana and the pineapple are often ingredients of *ganache* for delicious praline, or for the chocolate macaroons, of which the French *chocolatiers* are grand masters. Coconut on the other hand is suitable to accompany white chocolate, both in bars and in confectionary.

In France, generations of children have grown up drinking a cup of hot milk for breakfast in which soluble cocoa powder is dissolved with added banana and cereal flour: created in the early 20th century by the Banania brand, this is inspired by a traditional Nicaraguan mixture. In the United States, the *banana split* has always been a favorite dessert. Born in 1904 in Pennsylvania, it is simply a banana cut lengthwise, served with three scoops of ice cream and a topping of chocolate sauce.

The marriage between pears and chocolate is perhaps among the most successful, because the powerful taste of cocoa is not contrasted by the acidity of the fruit. The best-known specialty is the *Poire Belle Hélène* created around 1864 by Parisian chefs who took the cue from the Offenbach operetta: a cooked pear covered with chocolate sauce accompanied by a quenelle of vanilla ice cream and a dollop of whipped cream. Both in Italy and France, it is a tradition of many regions to prepare soft chestnut cakes with added cocoa powder or grated dark chocolate.

A very greedy social occasion is certainly the *Fondue au Chocolat*, a fondue that is prepared by warming in a bain-marie a mixture of liquid cream, butter, sugar and dark chocolate in pieces: it is placed in the center of the table on a plate warmer and the diners dip pieces of fresh fruit, such as strawberries, kiwi, bananas, pears, peaches and apricots, on long sticks.

Filled apricots are excellent, once cut in half and pitted, with a generous spoonful of gianduia cream.

Blackcurrants, raspberries, strawberries with their acidity are perfect to create contrasting notes in a praline, while the cherries under spirit are a must for an end of a meal *bon bon*.

Finally, even flowers can be used in this game of harmonies to give perfume and persistence to chocolate, among which orange and jasmine flowers. In Mexico, magnolia is added at the last moment to hot chocolate; in Romania rose is used for a jam; violets, crystallized with sugar elegantly decorate the cakes covered with dark icing. In the baroque cups of "Indian broth," the unmistakable scent of jasmine first conquered Florence and then the European courts.

GOURMAND
COFFEES

CHOCAVIAR COFFEE

1 ESPRESSO COFFEE
0.5 OZ (15 G) COCOA POWDER
1 OZ (30 G) GIANDUIA CREAM
2 FL OZ (60 ML) WHOLE FRESH MILK
1 0Z (30 G) CHOCAVIAR 75%

SERVES 1

In a small tray, place the Chocaviar in a uniform layer about 0.2 in (1/2 cm) high. With a teaspoon or a pastry brush, coat the outer edge of a punch glass in gianduia cream. Then dip it in the Chocaviar so that it is completely covered.

Heat the leftover gianduia cream in a lukewarm bain-marie and let it drip down the inner side of the glass, leaving a little on the bottom. Create a milk froth with the frother. Pour the espresso coffee into the glass and sprinkle a little cocoa powder over it. Then top it off with milk foam.

If you like, give another sprinkle of cocoa or drizzle of gianduia cream.

VENCHINO

1 FL OZ (30 ML) LIQUID FRESH CREAM
1 ESPRESSO COFFEE
3 GIANDUIOTTI
COCOA POWDER TO TASTE

SERVES 1

In a bowl, whisk the liquid cream with an electric whisk, until you get a shiny, slightly whipped but not buttery cream. Melt the Gianduiotti in a warm bain-marie or in the microwave and pour them in a perfect layer inside a glass cup. Over this velvety cream, pour an espresso coffee and then place a layer of whipped cream that slightly exceeds the edge of the cup. It will be even more delicious with a final sprinkling of cocoa powder.

CUBA RUM COFFEE

1 FL OZ (30 ML) AGED RUM
0.7 OZ (20 G) BROWN SUGAR
1 FL OZ (30 ML) SEMI-WHIPPED CREAM
1 LONG ESPRESSO COFFEE
0.35 OZ (10 G) CHOCAVIAR 75%

SERVES 1

Heat an Irish coffee glass, then pour in the rum and brown sugar: mix with a long spoon. Then, add the espresso and the semi-whipped cream, pouring them slowly along the back of a spoon. Sprinkle the surface with 1/2 tsp of Chocaviar.

DELICATE
HOT CHOCOLATE

17 FL OZ (500 ML) FRESH WHOLE MILK
3 OZ (90 G) DARK CHOCOLATE 75%
1.40 OZ (40 G) BITTER COCOA POWDER
1 0Z (30 G) BROWN SUGAR

SERVES 3

Break the chocolate into pieces: put it in a saucepan and melt it in a warm bain-marie, stirring with a wooden spoon. In a thick bottomed pan, pour the milk, the (sieved) cocoa powder and the sugar: mix vigorously with a small whisk. Put it on a low heat and keep stirring, bringing it almost to a boil. Take it off the heat for a few moments and then repeat the operation a second time. Turn off the heat and gradually incorporate the melted chocolate.

Amalgamate well and the warm, velvety chocolate will be ready to be tasted. For those who are milk intolerant, it is possible to replace the milk with water. In this case, first heat the water with the sugar, then add the cocoa while stirring and cook it in the same way as before, taking care to avoid the formation of lumps. Finally, incorporate the melted chocolate and allow it to thicken.

The recipe can also be made using only powders; in this case the doses will be: 17 fl oz (500 ml) milk; 3.5 oz (100 g) bitter cocoa powder; 1.7 oz (50 g) cane sugar; 0.7 oz (20 g) cornstarch.

RUM CUBANA

4.4 OZ (125 G) HOT CHOCOLATE
1 RUM CUBA CUNEESE
3.40 FL OZ (100 ML) WHIPPED CREAM
0.35 OZ (10 G) MERINGUE

SERVES 1

With a small knife, gently remove the bottom of a rum Cuneese, then with a spreading knife (or a pastry brush) remove the filling and spread it on the inside edge of a glass cup. Finely crumble the meringue, arrange it in a shallow dish and immerse the edge of the cup in it, making sure that it sticks to the glass.
Put the shell and the chocolate cap of the Cuneese in the cup and pour the hot chocolate on top. Garnish with a dollop of whipped cream and a pinch of meringue crumbs.

GIANDUIOTTA

4.4 OZ (125 G) HOT CHOCOLATE
5 GIANDUIOTTI

SERVES 1

Break up 4 Gianduiotti and put them in a pan: let them dissolve in a warm bain-marie, stirring with a wooden spoon, or in a microwave. Pour the mixture obtained in the glass cup. Then pour in the hot chocolate. Do not stir and, before serving, place the last whole gianduiotto on top, so that it can "sink" in this sweet sea.

CARAMELIZED NOUGATINE

4.2 OZ (120 G) HOT CHOCOLATE
0.7 OZ (20 G) GIANDUIA CREAM
4 NOUGATINE CHOCOLATES

SERVES 1

Unwrap the nougatines. With the help of a meat pounder, crush them on a chopping board covered with a cloth, until they are reduced to crumbs. Otherwise, pour in a non-stick pan 1 oz (30 g) sugar with a few drops of water: put on a low heat, let the sugar melt until sticky bubbles form. At this point incorporate 1 oz (30 g) hazelnut grains stirring continuously with a wooden spoon. When the sugar has dried, spread the mixture on a sheet of baking paper or on a marble surface: let it cool down and, when it is solid, crush it into crumbs.

With a teaspoon, spread the gianduia cream on the entire inner side and on the edge of a glass cup; then sprinkle completely with nougatine grain.

Finally, pour in the hot chocolate.

CREMINO CUT ESPRESSO

0.7 OZ (20 G) WHIPPED CREAM
0.7 OZ (20 G) PIEDMONT HAZELNUT GRAIN
1 LONG ESPRESSO COFFEE
GIANDUIA CREAM TO TASTE

FOR THE CREMINO ICE CREAM
11.30 OZ (320 G) FRESH WHOLE MILK
2.5 FL OZ (75 ML) FRESH LIQUID 35% FAT CREAM
2 OZ (60 G) HAZELNUT PASTE
3 OZ (90 G) SUCROSE
0.5 OZ (15 G) DEXTROSE
0.07 OZ (2 G) CAROB BEAN FLOUR
A PINCH OF SALT

SERVES 1

Prepare the hazelnut ice cream. In a large bowl with a hand whisk mix the milk, the cream, the dextrose, the sucrose, the carob flour and the salt. Once the ingredients are well blended, pour the mixture into a saucepan. Put it on a gentle heat and take it to 158 °F (70 °C), checking the temperature with a cooking thermometer. Then turn off the heat, place the pan in a cold water and ice bath to cool down. When it has reached the temperature of 122 °F (50 °C), incorporate the hazelnut paste, stir and let it cool again. Then pour it into the ice cream maker for about 30 min.

In a Martini cup, place a generous spoonful of ice cream, with a sac à poche create a swirl of whipped cream and garnish with gianduia cream.

Before serving, prepare the coffee and pour it gently into the cup.

VENCHI GOLD NUT MANHATTAN

5 OZ (140 G) HOT CHOCOLATE
1 OZ (30 G) GIANDUIA SPREAD
2 OZ (60 G) MANGO ICE CREAM
1 PIEDMONT TOASTED HAZELNUT
1 EDIBLE GOLD LEAF

SERVES 1

In a warm bain-marie, heat the gianduia spread, making it quite fluid. Pour it into a glass dessert bowl, then add the hot chocolate on top of it. Let it cool for a few minutes and then lay a scoop of mango ice cream (or, if you prefer, strawberry, stracciatella or ginger and cinnamon ice cream).

Decorate with a toasted hazelnut previously wrapped by hand in the edible gold leaf.

COOKING WITH
THE FOOD OF THE GODS

RECIPES BY RELAIS CUBA CHOCOLAT

FOIE GRAS CREMINO

SERVES 6

FOR THE CREMINO
4.2 OZ (120 G) FOIE GRAS
6.3 OZ (180 G) ENTRACQUE POTATOES
1 OZ (30 G) COCOA BUTTER
1.7 FL OZ (50 ML) COCCHI STORICO VERMOUTH
1 BAR OF DARK CHOCOLATE 75%
2 BAY LEAVES AND 1 CLOVE
COARSE SALT TO TASTE

FOR THE WAFER
1.8 OZ (50 G) RED BOILED BEANS
1.8 OZ (50 G) BORLOTTI BOILED BEANS
1 SHALLOT
0.7 OZ (20 G) COCOA BUTTER
1 CUP VEGETABLE BROTH
SALT AND PEPPER TO TASTE

PREPARATION TIME 50 MINUTES – TOTAL TIME 2 HOURS

For the cremino: cut the foie gras into chunks and sauté in a non-stick casserole with 0.7 oz (20 g) cocoa butter, bay leaves and clove. Pour in the vermouth and let it simmer. As soon as it is cooked, blend, sieve and incorporate the remaining cocoa butter in order to give solidity to the cream obtained. Cover the potatoes with coarse salt and bake them in the oven at 320 °F (160 °C) for 1 hour. Then peel them and, while still warm, mash them with the potato masher. Season with salt and pepper. Take a 7 in (18 cm) square mold, 1 in (3 cm) high (better use a silicone mold): with the help of a spatula, spread a first layer of liver pate 0.4 in (1 cm) high, then a layer 0.4 in (1 cm) of mashed potatoes and finally another layer of liver pate. Level well and put in the refrigerator to cool.

For the wafer: chop the shallot and lightly fry it with the cocoa butter, add the beans, pour in the vegetable broth, and cook for 20 minutes over low heat. When the beans are soft, blend them with a hand-blender. With a spatula, spread a thin layer on a sheet of baking paper cook at 356 °F (180 °C) for a few minutes, until it becomes a crispy wafer.

Take the cremino out of the oven and divide it into 6 equal parts. Place each square in a plate and finely grate dark chocolate over it. Accompany with a piece of crispy waffle.

CHOCAVIAR MINCE

SERVES 6

17 OZ (480 G) FASSONE BEEF FILLET
6 TSP CHOCAVIAR OR COCOA GRAINS
6 EGGS
6.3 OZ (180 G) TABLE SALT
4.2 OZ (120 G) SUGAR
1 BUNCH DANDELIONS
3 MONTEROSSO ANCHOVY FILLETS
2 OZ (60 G) BUTTER
3.5 OZ (100 G) BLU LANGHE SHEEP'S CHEESE
EXTRA VIRGIN OLIVE OIL TO TASTE
SALT AND PEPPER TO TASTE

PREPARATION TIME 15 MINUTES – TOTAL TIME 24 HOURS

Mix salt with sugar. Crack the eggs and keep the yolks, each in half the shell: lay them in a bowl, cover the yolks completely with the mixture of sugar and salt and leave to marinate for 24 hours until they have a solid-gummy consistency.

Cut the anchovies, stir in the butter and mix until you get a homogeneous cream: make 6 balls the size of a walnut.

On a chopping board, using a heavy knife, finely chop the meat. Place the meat in a bowl, add the chopped dandelion, a drizzle of extra virgin olive oil, salt, pepper and dress with the Chocaviar. Divide and arrange in each dish, using a round food mold 3 in (8 cm) in diameter.

Gently rinse the marinated egg under cold water to remove any residual sugar and salt and place it next to the meat, with a scoop of anchovy butter and two thin flakes of cheese.

WHITE
PISTACHIO BAR

SERVES 6

2.2 LB (1 KG) FRESH SPINACH
2.2 LB (1 KG) WHITE POTATOES
2.2 LB (1 KG) PURPLE POTATOES
4.4 LB (2 KG) COARSE SALT
8.8 OZ (250 G) ROBIOLA GOAT CHEESE OF ROCCAVERANO
3.5 OZ (100 G) SALTED WHITE CHOCOLATE
4.2 OZ (120 G) SHELLED BRONTE PISTACHIOS
4.2 OZ (120 G) COCOA BUTTER
1 TBSP FRESH THYME
EXTRA VIRGIN OLIVE OIL TO TASTE
SALT AND PEPPER TO TASTE

PREPARATION TIME 90 MINUTES

Put the potatoes in a baking dish, cover them with coarse salt and bake in the oven at 320 °F (160 °C) for 1 hour. While still warm, peel and crush the white potatoes with a fork, and dress with cocoa butter, salt and pepper. Repeat the operation with the purple potatoes, dressing them with cocoa butter and thyme. Steam-boil the spinach for a few minutes; drain, squeeze well, chop finely and season with extra virgin olive oil and salt. Toast the pistachios in the oven at 266 °F (130 °C) for 10 minutes, then, with a food processor, reduce them to grains. Break the white chocolate and melt it in a warm bain-marie. Then, using a small hand whisk, incorporate it into the robiola and make a well-blended cream.

In a 2 in (5 cm) high rectangular steel baking pan, with the help of a spatula, spread out, in layers: half the spinach, the purple potato puree, the robiola and chocolate cream, the white potato puree and finally the other half of spinach. Cover abundantly with pistachio grains. Place in the fridge until firm.

To serve, divide into 6 portions.

PIEDMONT TRIO

LA RUSS CHOCAVIAR

3.5 OZ (100 G) PEAS - 3.5 OZ (100 G) POTATOES - 3.5 OZ (100 G) CARROTS - 1 OZ (30 G) COOKED RED BEET-
ROOT - 3.5 OZ (100 G) TINNED TUNA IN BRINE - 3.5 OZ (100 G) THICK HOMEMADE MAYONNAISE -
1 TBSP WHITE VINEGAR - CHOCAVIAR 75 % OR COCOA GRAIN TO TASTE - TURMERIC AND SALT TO TASTE

PREPARATION TIME 30 MINUTES – TOTAL TIME 1 HOUR

Peel the carrots and potatoes and cut them into cubes. Together with the peas, put all the vegetables in the steam cooker for about 20 minutes, then let them cool. Peel the beetroot and cut into small cubes. Arrange all the vegetables in a salad bowl, add the chopped tuna and season with 1 tbsp vinegar and a pinch of curcuma and salt. Then, mix gently with the mayonnaise, incorporating a few chocaviar grains.

With the compound obtained, form small appetizer spheres.

NOCCIOLATA OF CELERY AND TOMA CHEESE

1 OZ (30 G) TOASTED AND SALTED PIEDMONT HAZELNUTS - 1 OZ (30 G) WHITE CHOCOLATE - 5.3 OZ (150 G)
HARD TOMA D'ALBA CHEESE - 3 STICKS OF CELERY - 1 ORGANIC LEMON - EXTRA VIRGIN OLIVE OIL TO TASTE
- SALT AND PEPPER TO TASTE

PREPARATION TIME 15 MINUTES – TOTAL TIME 15 MINUTES

Peel, destring and cut the celery into cubes. Cut the Toma into cubes, too. Cut the white chocolate into small flakes and crush the salted hazelnuts into grains. Assemble everything in a bowl and season with extra virgin olive oil, salt and grated lemon rind.

COLD VEAL IN TUNA SAUCE GRUÉ

14 OZ (400 G) FASSONE VEAL ROUND STEAK - 7 OZ (200 G) CANNED TUNA - 3 MONTEROSSO
ANCHOVIES IN SALT - 3 EGGS - 3 CAPERS IN SALT - 6 CAPER FLOWERS - 2 OZ (60 G) COCOA GRAIN GRUÉ -
EXTRA VIRGIN OLIVE OIL TO TASTE

PREPARATION TIME 40 MINUTES – TOTAL TIME 1 HOUR

Cook the meat pierced with a probe thermometer in the center in a vacuum oven at low temperature (118 °F/48 °C) for about 1 hour.

For the tuna sauce: hard boil the eggs and pass the yolks through a sieve: place them in a bowl, with a few drops of extra virgin olive oil and emulsify. Incorporate, the chopped tuna, capers and finely chopped anchovies a little at a time stirring with a wooden spoon. Work the mixture until you get a mayonnaise-like sauce.

Let the meat cool, then chop it with a large knife on a chopping board. Mix the tuna sauce with the meat, until a compact mixture is obtained. With this, form 6 small pears and, at the tip of each, put a caper flower. Lay a pear on each plate and cover it completely with cocoa grué.

CARNAROLI RISOTTO WITH DARK CHOCOLATE

SERVES 6

FOR THE STOCK
4.4 LB (2 KG) BEEF BONES
3.5 OZ (100 G) CARROTS
3.5 OZ (100 G) ONIONS
1 STICK CELERY
1.7 PT (1 L) RED WINE NEBBIOLO
1.7 OZ (50 G) ECUADOR DARK CHOCOLATE 100%
1/2 TSP NUTMEG
5 CLOVES
SALT AND PEPPER TO TASTE

FOR THE RISOTTO
17 OZ (480 G) CARNAROLI RICE
2 SHALLOTS
3.5 OZ (100 G) COCOA BUTTER
1 GLASS OF DRY WHITE WINE
3.5 PT (2 L) VEGETABLE STOCK
4 TBSP GRATED PARMIGIANO REGGIANO
2 ARTICHOKES, TRIMMED
SALT TO TASTE

PREPARATION TIME 40 MINUTES – TOTAL TIME 2 DAYS

Prepare the stock: Break the bones, put them in a saucepan with the spices and vegetables washed and sliced roughly. Sprinkle with 0.90 pt (1/2 l) red wine and cook in the oven at 212 °F (100 °C) for 12 hours. Transfer the pan to a low heat: incorporate the chocolate and pour in the remaining wine. Allow to evaporate, cover flush with hot water and continue cooking for another 6 hours. Filter well and put in the refrigerator to solidify for 6 hours: then remove the oily part on the surface. Put on the heat and reduce to 1/3 until you get a dense sauce.

Prepare the risotto: In a saucepan, soften the sliced shallots with 2 oz (60 g) cocoa butter; add the rice, toast it for a few moments and then blend it with the white wine. Add the boiling vegetable broth a little at a time and, stirring, add 6 tbsp stock. Cook the rice for 15 minutes, then remove from the heat and stir with 1.4 oz (40 g) cocoa butter and grated Parmigiano Reggiano.

Serve the risotto creating a heart of stock in the center. Serve garnished with thin slices of fried artichokes.

COCOA PLINZICOTTI

SERVES 6

FOR THE FILLING
27 OZ (200 G) MINCED BEEF
3.5 OZ (100 G) PORK SAUSAGE
3.5 OZ (100 G) PORK RIBS
2 TBSP GRATED PARMIGIANO
REGGIANO
6 TBSP STOCK (SEE RECIPE
ON PAGE 189)
2 GLASSES OF DRY WHITE WINE
A PINCH OF NUTMEG
2 CLOVES OF GARLIC
2 SPRIGS OF ROSEMARY
4 TBSP EXTRA VIRGIN OLIVE OIL
SALT AND PEPPER TO TASTE

FOR THE FRESH PASTA
13.4 OZ (380 G) ALL-PURPOSE FLOUR (TYPE 00)
2.8 OZ (80 G) DURUM WHEAT SEMOLINA
10 EGG YOLKS
0.30 OZ (8 G) COCOA POWDER
SALT TO TASTE

FOR DRESSING
1 BELL PEPPER
1 BROCCOLO
2 CARROTS
4 ASPARAGUS
3 CAULIFLOWER FLORETS
EXTRA VIRGIN OLIVE OIL TO TASTE

PREPARATION TIME 50 MINUTES – TOTAL TIME 2 HOURS

Prepare the stuffing: In a saucepan, brown the beef and the sausage with oil, garlic and rosemary; season with salt and pepper, pour in the wine and let it simmer. Add the ribs and continue cooking for a few minutes. With the help of a food processor, chop the meats adding the Parmigiano Reggiano, the stock and nutmeg.

Prepare the fresh pasta plinzicotti: Sift the flour and the cocoa powder on a pastry board creating a well and place the yolks in the center. Stir first with a fork and then knead vigorously with your hands until you make a smooth dough. Form a ball and let it rest for 30 minutes in the fridge, covered with a towel. Then, with a rolling pin roll out the dough to a thin sheet, from which you will cut 3 cm squares. At the center of each, put about a nut of filling, fold the pastry and seal with the dough wheel, pinching the corners with your hands.

Prepare the vegetables for dressing: Wash and cut the vegetables into cubes: put them in the special basket of the steam cooker and let them cook. Then sauté in a frying pan with 2 tablespoons of oil.

Boil the cocoa plinzicotti in salted water for 3 minutes: drain and pour into the pan with the vegetables. Let them absorb the flavor for 1 minute and then serve.

KING PRAWNS & CHOCAVIAR

SERVES 6

2 POMEGRANATES
6 KING PRAWNS
7 OZ (200 G) BURRATA
1 ORGANIC LEMON
5 TBSP CHOCAVIAR
0.5 OZ (15 G) AGAR AGAR
1 SPRIG OF FRESH THYME

PREPARATION TIME 20 MINUTES – TOTAL TIME 4 HOURS

Open the pomegranates, take out the seeds and blend them. Pass the juice obtained through a fine mesh sieve, perfume it with the thyme and dissolve the agar agar by stirring it in. Distribute the mixture in 6 round molds 0.4 in (1 cm) high and put them in the refrigerator to harden for at least 3-4 hours. Season the center of the burrata with a little grated lemon peel.

Shell the prawns by gently removing the shell and spinal cord.

To serve, remove the medallions of pomegranate jelly from the refrigerator, take them out of the molds and put them on plates. On top, place 1 spoon of burrata and 1 prawn on which you will sprinkle a bit of grated lemon zest.

Sprinkle some Chocaviar all over the plate.

SHRIMP NOCCIOLATA

SERVES 6

18 FRESH SHRIMP
2 EGGS
5.3 OZ (150 G) TOASTED PIEDMONT HAZELNUTS
1.8 OZ (50 G) RICE FLOUR
12 OZ (350 G) LENTILS
1.7 PT (1 L) VEGETABLE BROTH
1.8 OZ (50 G) COCOA GRAIN
2 OZ (60 G) COCOA BUTTER
1 SPRIG OF FRESH THYME
1 PIECE OF FRESH GINGER
1 ORGANIC LEMON
SALT AND PEPPER TO TASTE
VEGETABLE OIL FOR FRYING TO TASTE

PREPARATION TIME 30 MINUTES – TOTAL TIME 1 HOUR

In a pan, toast the lentils with 1.4 oz (40 g) cocoa butter, season with the aromas, then cover with the vegetable stock and cook for 25 minutes. When they start to dissolve, remove them from the heat, let them cool down and then with a hand blender whisk them into a velvety cream. Keep them warm.

Clean the shrimp by removing the head, legs and shell: wash and dry them. In a deep dish, beat the eggs. Place the hazelnuts into a food processor: whisk half until you get a grain and the other half until you have a fine flour. Mix the rice flour with the hazelnut and dip the shrimp in this. Then immerse them in the eggs and finally dip into the hazelnut grains. Season with salt and pepper.

In a large pan, heat the oil adding some cocoa butter. Dip the prawns and fry until brown. Then let them dry on oil-absorbing cooking paper and then stick them on wooden skewers.

On each plate, put 2 tbsp of lentil cream and then place a fried shrimp on top. Sprinkle with cocoa grain and serve.

GUINEA FOWL
IN GIANDUIA POLENTA

SERVES 6

6 GUINEA FOWL LEGS
17 OZ (480 G) ORGANIC CORN FLOUR
3.5 OZ (100 G) COCOA BUTTER
1 BUNCH OF RED RADICCHIO
2.6 PT (1.5 L) WATER
3 GIANDUIOTTI
1 ORGANIC ORANGE
3.5 OZ (100 G) COCOA GRAIN
1 BUNCH OF FRESH THYME
2 TBSP EXTRA VIRGIN OLIVE OIL
SALT AND PEPPER TO TASTE

PREPARATION TIME 2 HOURS 30 MINUTES – TOTAL TIME 2 HOURS 50 MINUTES

In a pot bring the water to a boil, add salt, add 2 tbsp of extra virgin olive oil and then take off the heat. Sprinkle in the cornmeal stirring energetically with a hand whisk. Cook for 90 minutes. At the end of the cooking process, distribute it in 6 individual molds, previously brushed with cocoa butter and sprinkled with cocoa grains. At the heart of each one lay 1/2 gianduiotto.

Bone the guinea-fowl legs, beat them with a pounder and fill them with sliced red radicchio, a drop of extra virgin olive oil, 1/2 teaspoon cocoa grain and a grated orange peel. Season with salt, pepper and sprinkle with fresh thyme.

Melt the remaining cocoa butter in a bain-marie or in microwave and brush the surface of the meat. Place each leg inside an oven cocotte to give them a round shape. Cook in the oven at 374 °F (190 °C) for 15 minutes; at the same time, bake the individual polenta molds. Take out of the molds and, while still hot, serve the polenta gianduiotto patties with the guinea fowl legs.

COCOA
HEART FILLET

SERVES 6

6 MEDALLIONS OF BEEF FILLET
5 MEDIUM SIZED POTATOES
5.3 OZ (150 G) COCOA BUTTER
12 TBSP COCOA STOCK (SEE RECIPE ON PAGE 189)
1 FL OZ (30 ML) BRANDY
2 SPRIGS OF ROSEMARY
SALT AND PEPPER TO TASTE

PREPARATION TIME 25 MINUTES – TOTAL TIME 40 MINUTES

Peel, wash and slice the potatoes into 1/4 in (1/2 cm) thick slices. Cook in a large pan with rosemary and cocoa butter until brown. Take off the heat and keep warm.

Take the slices of meat and rub them with 1.8 oz (50 g) cocoa butter, previously melted in a bain-marie, season with salt and pepper.

Put the remaining cocoa butter in a non-stick frying pan and let it warm on a low heat perfuming it with rosemary. Add the slices of beef and cook them by browning on both sides, but turning them only once. Pour in the brandy and let it evaporate.

In the meantime, heat the stock. To serve, place a medallion of meat in each plate, sprinkled with 2 spoons of stock and surrounded with potato slices.

SUPREME TEAR

SERVES 6

6 OZ (175 G) DARK CHOCOLATE 75%
4.4 OZ (125 G) COW'S BUTTER
3.9 OZ (110 G) SUGAR
1 OZ (30 G) SUPREME GIANDUIA SPREAD
1 OZ (30 G) ALL-PURPOSE FLOUR (TYPE 00)
3 EGGS
6 TBSP CUSTARD

PREPARATION TIME 30 MINUTES – TOTAL TIME 45 MINUTES

With an electric whisk, beat the eggs with the sugar, until you get a light and fluffy mixture. Incorporate the sifted flour a little at a time and stir with a hand whisk until a smooth mixture is obtained. Put the butter and the chopped chocolate in a pan: melt over a bain-marie or in a microwave on minimum power. Once the chocolate is melted, let it cool down and then add it to the beaten egg.

Butter 6 round molds (silicone molds are preferable) up to 3/4 from the edge and pour up to half the prepared mixture. Place a tsp of gianduia cream in the center of each and pass them in a preheated oven at 374 °F/ 392°F (190 °C/200 °C) for 10 minutes.

Once taken out of the oven, let the cakes cool down and then take them out of the molds. Serve them with a spoonful of custard flavored with orange juice.

TARTUFATA
TORRON GIANDUIA

SERVES 6

8.8 OZ (250 G) DARK CHOCOLATE 75%
7 OZ (200 G) ALL-PURPOSE FLOUR (TYPE 00)
4 FL OZ (120 ML) FRESH MILK
5.3 OZ (150 G) FRESH WHIPPED CREAM
3.5 OZ (100 G) CRUMBLY TORRONE
3.5 OZ (100 G) GIANDUIOTTI
3.5 OZ (100 G) COWS' BUTTER
3.5 OZ (100 G) SUGAR
1 SACHET OF BAKING POWDER
4 EGGS

PREPARATION TIME 50 MINUTES – TOTAL TIME 90 MINUTES

In a thick bottomed pan, placed in a warm bain-marie, melt the butter and the chocolate, stirring with a wooden spoon. Then, add the previously heated milk, a little at a time, and mix until a cream is obtained.

Crack the eggs, separate the egg yolks from the egg whites and whip the latter until firm. Blend the egg yolks with the sugar and then gently add them to the chocolate cream. Sift the flour with the yeast and, little at a time, with a hand whisk, incorporate it into the egg and chocolate mixture. Finally, add the egg whites with slow movements from the bottom to the top.

Butter and flour a cake tin and gently pour in the mixture: cook in a pre-heated oven at 356 °F (180 °C) for about 20 minutes. Take the cocoa sponge out of the tin and turn it upside down to allow it to cool.

Crush the nougat into small chunks with a meat tenderizer and mix it with whipped cream. With this mixture fill the cake cut in half.

On a sheet of baking paper or on a cold marble surface, spread thin strips of chocolate – made with the previously melted gianduiotti – with a steel spatula: let them cool well. Then remove them, using the spatula, to obtain some gianduia strips to decorate the cake.

COCKTAIL TIME
RECIPES BY RELAIS CUBA CHOCOLAT

CUBA
SPRITZ

1 PART OF RED VERMOUTH
1 PART OF APERITIVO LUXARDO
3 PARTS OF SPUMANTE BRUT
0.07 OZ (2 G) CHOCAVIAR
1 RED VERMOUTH GELÈE

Place some ice cubes in a wine goblet, add the vermouth, then the sparkling brut and finally the Aperitivo Luxardo, pouring it with a circular movement.
Mix with a cocktail spoon. Drop in the Chocaviar and attach the vermouth gelèe on the edge of the glass.
Serve with a double straw so as to avoid the ice when drinking and aspirate the Chocaviar microspheres, which will make the tasting even more special.

VENCHI
WATERFALL

3.4 FL OZ (100 ML) BRUT SPARKLING WINE
1 SALTED WHITE CHOCOLATE TRUFFLE
0.1 OZ (3 G) CHOCAVIAR 75%

Place the Chocaviar in a goblet. Pour in the sparkling wine. Stick the salted truffle on the edge of the glass and serve.

This pairing will surprise you, transforming the tasting experience into a harmony of flavors. The Chocaviar clings to the perlage, rises up the glass and then cascades down in a waterfall effect several times.

The chocolate binds to the vanilla notes of the oak in which the sparkling wine has been refined. The taste is balanced, the Brut turns into a Satèn and the truffle, made with cocoa, milk, hazelnuts, almonds and roasted and salted pistachios, gives tasty notes that conquer the palate.

ALCOHOL
CAROUSEL

2 OZ (60 ML) BARBERA D'ASTI
1 OZ (30 ML) CAMPARI
1 OZ (30 ML) TASSONI CEDRATA
1 CUBE OF CHEESE
1 CUBE OF DARK CHOCOLATE

In a tumbler pour first the Barbera, then the Campari and finally the Cedrata. Mix well and serve with a cube of 60% dark chocolate and a cube of Piedmontese Toma or a little aged PDO Ra-schera.

This "Futurist Polydrink," originally called *Giostra D'alcol*, dates back to the 1930s and was cre-ated during the Manifesto of Futurist cuisine.

In this interpretation, the Carousel is inspired by the "tail" to be grasped on carnival swing rides: the original version includes two long toothpicks, spiking cubes of chocolate and cheese.

THE DARK
BEYOND THIRST

1.5 OZ (45 ML) DOPO TEATRO COCCHI VERMOUTH
0.7 OZ (20 ML) YOUNG GRAPPA
0.3 OZ (10 ML) RABARBARO ZUCCA
1 DARK NAPOLITAIN AT 75%

Fill the tumbler with ice cubes. Pour, in sequence, the vermouth, the grappa and the Rabarbaro Zucca. Mix with a cocktail spoon.

Fasten a dark napolitain to the edge of the glass using a drop of chocolate as glue, to enhance the notes of rhubarb and vermouth.

CHOCO NEGRONI

1 FL OZ (30 ML) GIN
1 FL OZ (30 ML) CAMPARI
1 FL OZ (30 ML) STORICO COCCHI VERMOUTH
1 TSP DARK GIANDUIA SPREAD
1 TSP CHOCAVIAR
1 VERMOUTH GELÈE

Decorate the edge of the tumbler with the gianduia cream and sprinkle on the Chocaviar. Put an ice cube in it and prepare the Negroni, mixing the ingredients directly in the glass with a cocktail spoon.
Attach the vermouth gelèe to the edge of the glass and serve.

MEDI-TEA-TION
ALL DAY FIZZ

1.35 FL OZ (40 ML) MEZCAL
0.30 FL OZ (10 ML) BRANDY
0.5 FL OZ (15 ML) AGAVE SYRUP
0.30 FL OZ (10 ML) EGG WHITE
0.1 OZ (3 G) CHINESE PU'ERH BLACK TEA (FERMENTED)
1 GIANDUIOTTO

Pour into the shaker the young mezcal, the Italian brandy, the agave syrup and the pasteurized egg whites and shake vigorously without ice in order to allow the egg whites to mix well; then add some crushed ice and continue to shake. Pour through a sieve into the glass and then incorporate a splash (final foam) of tea soda.

To prepare the tea soda, leave 2/3 g of leaves in infusion for 4 minutes in 5 fl oz (150 ml) of water at 203 °F (95 °C). Let it cool down and then put it into a siphon to turn it into soda.

This cocktail won the first prize at the Tea Master Cup Italia 2018 on the Mont Blanc. It is perfect to sip with a gianduiotto.

CHOCOLATE SOMMELIER

CREMINO'S

1 FL OZ (30 ML) CUBAN RUM
0.70 FL OZ (20 ML) VODKA
0.3FL OZ (10 ML) ESPRESSO COFFEE
1 FL OZ (30 ML) HAZELNUT LIQUOR

FOR THE HAZELNUT LIQUOR
17 FL OZ (500 ML) FRESH WHOLE MILK
17 FL OZ (500 ML) FRESH LIQUID CREAM
17.5 OZ (500 G) HAZELNUT PASTE
9.5 OZ (270 G) PURE ALCOHOL

For the hazelnut liquor: heat the milk with the cream, then, stirring well, incorporate the hazelnut paste a little at a time. Place on a gentle heat and bring to a boil. Switch off and let it cool down. Then, incorporate the alcohol and stir well. With a fine mesh sieve, filter and pour into a bottle: put it in the refrigerator or in a cool place for 2 weeks. For the Cremino's: in a high glass pour the Cuban rum, then the hazelnut liquor and finally the coffee and vodka previously mixed together.
The layers of varying intensity will offer a pleasant surprise to your taste buds.

The publisher would like to thank **VENCHI** and **GIOVANNI BATTISTA MAN-TELLI** for the precious and indispensable collaboration in realizing this volume, the result of a life dedicated to the love of chocolate in all its solid, liquid, hot, cold and creamy forms. Without their passion, competence and availability this book would not have seen the light. A heartfelt thanks also goes to all the people who made the photographic sessions at the Cuneo company possible and in particular to all the staff of the **RELAIS CUBA CHOCOLAT OF CUNEO**, that is, Luke and Khadija for the cocktail chapter, chef Silvana and Beppe, Vivian, Daniela, Mirosa, Tiziana and Cristina for the chocolaterie and pastry chapter, Domenica and Sonia for the *mis en place* of the dishes, and Simona and Imad for the cafeteria chapter.

ALPHABETICAL INDEX
OF RECIPE INGREDIENTS